Gifted

Gifted

An Extraordinary Journey
Through Illness and
Liver Transplantation

Dan Bonner

Foreword By
Elizabeth Ryan, RN, BSN, CCTN
The Hospital of the University of Pennsylvania

Two Harbors Press

Copyright © 2011 by Dan Bonner.

Two Harbors Press
212 3rd Avenue North, Suite 290
Minneapolis, MN 55401
612.455.2293
www.TwoHarborsPress.com

All rights reserved. No part of this publication may be reproduced,
stored in a retrieval system, or transmitted, in any form or by any
means, electronic, mechanical, photocopying, recording, or otherwise,
without the prior written permission of the author.

ISBN-13: 978-1-937293-83-3
LCCN: 2011943516

Distributed by Itasca Books
Elizabeth Ryan, RN, BSN, CCTN, The Hospital of the University of
Pennsylvania

Editing services provided by Caroline Pastore of The Well Turned
Phrase Writing and Editing Services (email: thewellturnedphrase@
gmail.com)

Back cover photograph provided by Bethany Bearmore of Bethany
Bearmore Photography (www.bethanybearmorephotography.com/blog)

Front and back cover design provided by Chris Koehler of Great
Point Media Design (www.greatpointmediadesign.com)

Public Relations and Marketing Manager, Lori Santucci.

Typeset by Steve Porter

Printed in the United States of America

Contents

Preface

WHILE THIS BOOK IS intended to be inspirational, it also deals with involved medical terms, conditions, and treatments. My first suggestion, if you have medically related questions, is to speak to a trusted physician. The onset of a serious medical illness can be an experience that proves vice-like in its grip of fear and confusion. However, I have found that educating oneself is the best defense against feelings of helplessness and fright, in addition to maintaining a tight support circle of friends and family. While I can provide you with a personal perspective on illness, I am not a physician.

Ulcerative colitis (UC) is the first condition that appears in this book. It is a digestive disorder that affects the intestines in one of three ways: a portion of the intestine, one half of the intestine, or the entire intestine. If it appears in one half of the intestine, imagine a drinking straw cut in half lengthways: one half of the straw would be affected and the other would not. Symptoms include abdominal pain, increased bowel movements and bloody diarrhea. It is usually diagnosed by a colonoscopy, a procedure that involves the insertion of a small tube equipped with a camera guided from the rectum into the intestines. There is no cure for UC, but it can be controlled with various medications depending on how severe the individual case is. UC also puts the affected person at an increased risk for colon cancer. It is my understanding that the incidence of occurrence of UC in the United States is less than 100 people per 100,000.

After trying several rounds of medications, the one that worked best for me is called Mercaptopurine, or 6 MP for short. 6 MP is a low-dose, oral form of chemotherapy (chemo) that is used to prevent the growth of pre-cancerous cells in the body. Since 6 MP is a form of chemo, I was forced to have blood drawn every three months to monitor the other organs in my body to ensure that the 6 MP was not having a detrimental effect on my system.

I never understood the results of my blood work in the beginning—it was only after I began having true issues with my liver that I vigorously researched the meaning behind all those cryptic-looking tables of numerical data. Specifically, doctors were looking at my liver enzymes AST, ALT, GGT, and Alk Phos. These enzymes tell a collective story about how well the liver is functioning and what might be wrong. I later was introduced to bilirubin or "bili," which I understood to be a toxic chemical that is a byproduct of the liver excreted in stool. When my liver was not functioning properly, bili backed up into my bloodstream causing me to become jaundice, which is a yellowing of the eyes and skin. It was ultimately through blood work results that I discovered there was a problem.

In order to diagnose what was wrong with my liver, I had to go through a procedure called "ERCP" which stands for Endoscopic Retrograde Cholangio-pancreatogram. This procedure involves the insertion of a camera-equipped tube down the throat that is then navigated to the liver where a dye is injected and images of the liver are taken. It was this procedure that confirmed my diagnosis of Primary Sclerosing Cholangitis (PSC).

PSC is a disease in which the passageways of the liver, called bile ducts, progressively close. Over time, the passageways become so tightly shut that the liver cannot function properly. Left untreated, PSC will ultimately cause liver failure and death. The only "cure" for PSC is liver transplantation. It is my understanding that the incidence of occurrence of PSC in the United States is less than two people per 100,000.

Throughout the book I try to explain these conditions and terms to the best of my ability. Too often we (as I did) become lost in the seeming sea of numbers and terms that often accompany chronic physical illness. My goal is for you, the reader, to move through the pages with ease and to leave, if I've done my job well, with a deeper layman understanding of UC and PSC. If I've done my job as well as I ideally would like to, you'll also leave with a sense of inspiration, a smile, and maybe even a laugh or two.

I reiterate my earlier encouragement that you speak to a physician for a professional opinion concerning any medical questions. I made it a point to learn and absorb as much information as I could about my illnesses so that I might ask educated questions of the doctors. I also felt that through education, I was preparing myself physically and mentally for whatever the future of the illness might hold. My main source of information was usually the internet. While the internet does contain a wealth of information, it can be frustrating to the point of despair when you don't know what you are seeking—a scenario with which I was well familiar.

With that, I would like to thank you, with a heart of true gratitude, for choosing to read my book. Writing it was in itself a gift that filled me with hope and inspiration. I hope that you feel as gifted as I do when you finish reading it. Much love always!

<u>Foreword</u>

AFTER NINE YEARS AS a surgical unit nurse at The Hospital of the University of Pennsylvania, a former patient and now dear friend, Dan Bonner, requested that I write the foreword for his first book.

At first, the task seemed overwhelming. Having never written anything of significance regarding my career, I found it difficult to describe the special nurse-patient dynamic and my relationship to this individual, who has inspired me to be a better mother, wife, nurse and person. Over the past few months while pondering how to explain this and reflect upon how caring for him has impacted my life as a nurse, I was surprised at what I realized.

Every morning in Rhoads 4, the organ transplant nursing unit, the night nurses sign off on a report to the day nurse: a summary of the patient's progress throughout the night. As a novice nurse in 2002, I was handed a report on a patient near my age that had just undergone a Cholecystectomy (gallbladder removal). I was intimidated, knowing that this particular surgery required a myriad of tubes passing in and out of the patient's body. It was then that I met Dan Bonner, put on my game face and tried my best to ease some of his anxiety through teaching, explaining and offering support as he recovered. It was clear that he needed someone he could trust to guide him through this. Over the next few days I met Dan's family who are also lovely individuals. It was apparent that there was something very special about them, and about this patient.

After having discharged Dan, I often prayed for him to receive a good liver. I knew that I'd see him again. This was very odd behavior for me, a person who never brought my work home, whether it be physical or emotional. I'm the type of nurse who goes to work, does my job to the best of my ability, and returns home to my family thinking nothing about the day at the hospital.

In early 2005, I ran into Dan again and learned that he was suffering from the end stages of liver disease. Soon thereafter I saw his name on our admissions box one fine morning with a report that he had received the liver transplant for which he'd been waiting so long! I believe that I speak for all nurses when I say that the average patient is not so much forgotten by the nurse, but becomes a very distant memory over the years. It is indeed the rare occasion when a patient in my profession remains close to you after discharge, is always remembered in your prayers and becomes a friend. When receiving word of them or their family, your heart smiles.

Working with and caring for Dan and his family over the years has been an extremely rewarding experience for me. His wife, Sue, is an inspiration to us all for the amount of love, devotion, support, and courage that she has given Dan over the course of his illness and recovery. Sue makes me want to be a better wife. Every time I was in his Aunt Marg's presence or had my arm around her shoulder, I felt the worry for her nephew and her unconditional love for him. She made me realize that in times of illness and disease, it is also the family members of the patient who need care and support.

I have often asked myself why, in my nine years of nursing, there are so few who have had such a profound effect on me. I reasoned that it could be factors such as common interests or age that form the bond of friendship. Sometimes, there is no explanation and I accept that. The memory of these patients I carry with me throughout my career. They are the ones who touch my heart and remind me why I am an Organ Transplant Nurse and why I chose nursing as my career path. They became, unexpectedly, a part of my life. We often share warm reunions alongside our families at Organ Transplant Fundraisers. The gratitude I feel from knowing them reaffirms why I do what I do in being a nurse—to help others, aid in their recuperation and offer support when it is needed. Dan is and always will be a dear friend and an inspiration to my life and career. I will always pray for his health and be there for him and his family. When our paths crossed, I became a better nurse and I grew as an individual. For that I am truly thankful.

After having read this book, I can say with complete honesty that I have never met a more courageous, reflective and spiritual man than Dan. This book was not only educational, but helped me as a person and a nurse to be more mindful of what my patients have endured emotionally during their battles with physical, life-threatening illness. It also reminds the reader how tragedy can strike even the most average, normal family, displays unconditional love at its best, and attests to the power of God and all His miracles.

This work captures the life of a man with a serious illness, the processes of organ transplantation and recovery, and a patient's view of healthcare. If you or someone that you know are dealing with organ failure, a chronic illness, or are interested in the organ transplant process, this story will offer intriguing insight. If you are a healthcare professional, this book may help you to "step into the shoes of the patient" and enhance your practice by considering what people have experienced in their lives before they become a patient of yours.

Elizabeth Ryan, RN, BSN, CCTN
The Hospital of the University of Pennsylvania
Staff Nurse, Surgical Nursing
Rhoads 4

GIFTED

This book is dedicated to my girl, Susie.
My life is infinitely better with you in it.
I love you more than life itself.

Chapter 1:
Crazy Thursdays

WHILE SUE AND I were dating but living together, we made it a habit of holding a date night each week on Thursday, calling it, "Crazy Thursday." We went out to eat, eating whatever we wanted so long as it was fun, with absolutely no calorie counting. That particular Thursday, we had just gotten home from our eating frenzy and decided to watch some TV before going to bed. While lounging on the couch, I felt a pain shooting through my liver that caused me to fidget, but nothing more severe. Sue asked if I was ok, and I told her I had some pain in my liver, but just needed to get comfortable. Sue accepted this and quickly fell asleep. After tucking her in, as was our routine with whoever was the first to go to bed, I returned to the couch, still trying to find a comfortable position to lie in.

I watched an episode of "ER" but was uncomfortable the whole time as the pain in my liver had become far more considerable. I was dog tired and didn't want to wake Sue with my continual squirming so I attempted to sleep on the couch. One hour passed, then another, and another, as the level of pain in my liver reached a degree I had never before experienced. My eyes welled with tears as I slowly paced our small New York City apartment from our econo-sized living room, down a narrow hallway into the kitchen, and back again trying to find some level of comfort in walking. Unable to find any relief from the pain, I knew something was wrong.

I woke Sue around 2:00 a.m. and told her what was happening. She asked, "How long has this been going on?" I said, "Ever since we laid on the couch to watch TV. It's never been this bad before so I think I should give UPenn (this is how my family and friends referred to the Hospital of the University of Pennsylvania or HUP) a call."

Sue agreed. I called the hospital and had the gastroenterologist on duty paged. Shortly thereafter, the gastro returned my call and asked how I was doing. I explained that I had Primary Schlerosing Cholangitis (PSC), was listed for a liver transplant with UPenn, was in a tremendous amount of pain and needed guidance. The gastroenterologist gave me the option of driving down to UPenn, but encouraged me to go to my local emergency room if I was in such severe pain. "Ok, thanks." I said, and hung up the phone, feeling unsure of my next move.

I told Sue what the doctor had said, and she again asked what I thought we should do. It was a risk, I thought, to drive to the local emergency room, since the most likely scenario would be the administration of a pain killer, followed by an even more drawn-out transport to UPenn. We agreed to make the drive to UPenn even though the pain I was feeling was well beyond my own personal pain threshold and a local emergency room could take it away much sooner. We put some clothes on and began the long drive down to UPenn. It was 4:30 a.m. on Friday, March 11, 2005.

Sue retrieved the car and pulled up to the front of our apartment. I had difficulty walking as the pain was intense but slowly made my way downstairs. When I opened the door to go outside, the cool, March air excited my lungs as if I were about to go on one of the early morning runs I was able to embark on only weeks earlier. I climbed into the backseat of the car with every intention of trying to sleep, or at least lie down. I couldn't do either as my liver felt as though it were stabbing me from the inside. I tried everything twice: sitting straight up, leaning on my left side, my right side, and getting on all fours. I found comfort only momentarily before the pain in my liver would lash out, reverberating through my entire body and forcing me to move yet again. After seeking some sort of repose but never finding it, I became nauseous from the pain and closed my eyes to try to hold back the inevitable regurgitation.

Sue called out to me, "How are you doing, Honey?" I replied, "I'm ok," not wanting her to worry. However, I knew that I was going to throw up any second, so I yelled to Sue, "I have to throw up so I'm going to stick my head out the window." Sue said, "Do you want me to pull over?" I yelled, "No! Just keep driving but see if you can get into the slow lane." As soon as Sue made it into the slow lane, I opened the back window, stuck my head out as far as I could, and disgorged everything in my system. The vomiting was so forceful that I swore my stomach was lying somewhere on the New Jersey Turnpike around exit 7A, the exit for Six Flags Great Adventure. A "great adventure" indeed... After spitting out any remaining remnants of dinner, I pulled my head back into the car and tried to relax. I did find temporary relief from the pain in my liver, but within minutes it returned with vengeance. The pain hit hard initially, causing me to lose my breath. I gave up trying to find a comfortable position and instead focused on my breathing. After trying several breathing techniques, the only technique that worked was taking short, quick breaths. I felt myself become lightheaded a few times and so had to slow my breathing down but overall, it worked well.

The drive to UPenn seemed to take forever despite the fact that it was very early in the morning and there was no traffic on the roads. When Sue pulled in front of the emergency room, I guessed we had been in the car for at least four hours; in reality, it had only been two.

When I walked into the dimly lit emergency room, one person was in the process of checking in and another two, who looked like a couple, were sitting in the waiting area. I stopped at the first seat in the room and knelt down next to it, holding the arm just to maintain my balance. I waited until the person before me was done checking in and then I made my way over to that seat. It took quite a while to stand up, regain my balance, and shuffle over to the chair. I gingerly sat down and blurted out my situation in two breaths: "Hi my name is Dan Bonner and I'm on the transplant waiting list for a liver. I paged the gastro on duty and drove down here. On a scale of 1 to 10 my pain is a 12." The person behind the desk, most likely a nurse, immediately stood and brought me a wheelchair. After helping me into the wheelchair, the nurse then brought me to the first open room on the floor. According to my medical records, I was triaged at 6:29 a.m. and registered by 6:37 a.m. My blood pressure was 140/66, my heart rate was 75, my temperature was 96.8, and my pain was a 9 (I guess they can't record a 12 on a 10 scale).

After the nurse helped me into bed, Sue walked through the door with another nurse right behind her. The nurse began asking questions concerning my situation and I said to her in short, quick breaths, "I have a liver disease, and I'm listed through HUP to get a liver. I paged the gastro on duty several hours ago who told me to go to my local ER. I thought coming here was a better idea. On a scale of 1 to 10, my pain is a 12 so I need a painkiller. Also, morphine doesn't do anything for me so I'm going to need Demerol or whatever the equivalent of Demerol is you carry (due to an increase in patients experiencing allergic reactions to Demerol, some hospitals, HUP being one of them, no longer uses Demerol as an opioid.) I know you'll need to get a doctor's permission to give me the painkiller so I would appreciate it if you could track the doctor down as soon as possible." Having been in and out of hospitals for years, I was well-versed in disease treatment and hospital protocol. The nurse was momentarily stunned by my proficiency but recovered quickly, said, "Ok." and immediately left the room.

Minutes later, the doctor entered with the same nurse. He had only glanced at me before saying, "Get this guy what he needs." It was obvious the nurse had briefed him on my condition, since there was no other way he would have given out a narcotic so freely; but my banana-yellow skin and eyes confirmed my story was accurate. After the nurse had left to gather an IV set-up, I explained, as well as I could, more about my reasons for being there and my ongoing condition.

He said, "Well, we'll get the painkiller into you right away and then we'll take it from there. I'll also try to get in touch with gastroenterology and see who spoke with you. Hang in there, Mr. Bonner; we'll take that pain away for you in no time." The nurse quickly returned, set up an IV, and injected the Demerol equivalent pain killer, most likely, Dilaudid. I felt the drug hit my bloodstream and the pain subside immediately. I felt like a hardcore junkie getting his fix, losing sense of reality, and relaxing on a fluffy cloud.

Aunt Marg walked in moments later while Sue and I were waiting to hear what the next steps would be. Aunt Marg is my Dad's sister who lived near UPenn in Philadelphia and always kept close tabs on me. I was not surprised to see her at the hospital in such a short amount of time as word spreads so quickly in my family when someone is in trouble. As I was telling her what happened, the gastroenterologist I had spoken with during the night came into the room. He said he was surprised to see me, having thought I would have chosen to go to my local emergency room. I explained to him that most of the hospitals would have just stuck a band-aid on me then sent me to UPenn anyway, so I was simply removing the middle man. He seemed genuinely concerned that I had been in pain for as long as I had to endure to ride to the hospital, but said he felt I had made the best decision. He then informed me that I was being admitted and moved to a more comfortable room. He also said that he would alert the transplant unit and pre-transplant physician. "It's Dr. Burke," I said, and he made a note of it, said someone would contact her, and then he left. A nurse appeared shortly thereafter to draw blood. I knew they were going to check my liver enzymes to see how they compared to my previous doctor's visit in February. It was no surprise that my liver had worsened considerably, and was, in fact, barely functioning.

I was eventually moved to a room in a section of the hospital with which I was unfamiliar. My roommate was a large, mentally disturbed man, about 6'4," who claimed that he was owed $75.00. As he became increasingly agitated that he was not paid his $75.00, I felt it was in my best interest to be moved to another room; my request was granted, fortunately, and I was moved to another room on the same floor, this time with no roommate.

Dr. Burke visited later to discuss her plans for me. She wanted me to have a specific test aimed at determining the level at which my liver was actually functioning or not functioning. The only problem, she said, was that the machine was booked for the rest of the day, so she was trying to squeeze me in later in the day with a worse-case scenario of Saturday. I surmised the test would reveal how critical it was for me to undergo the transplant. Dr. Burke returned later in the day to inform me that I would not be going for the test on Friday and that she was sorry. She said she would see to it personally that I was scheduled for Saturday despite the fact that there was no room for additional appointments. After asking if I needed anything further, she said goodbye for the night.

It was now 7:00 p.m. Our journey to UPenn began at 4:30 a.m. that morning; I had been continuously moved from one place to another, and I was exhausted. I was given permission to eat, so Sue ventured out to pick up some sandwiches from Boston Market, as we had missed dinner service. While we ate, I received a visit from one of my liver transplant surgeons, Dr. Frank. It was good to see him, since I hadn't spoken to him since my pre-transplant evaluation in August of 2004. Dr. Frank explained why it was taking a long time for my transplant to move ahead due to some unique circumstances. On paper, I had been in need of a transplant for a considerable amount of time. However, I was in excellent physical shape for someone who, on paper, was as sick as I was. Because I was able to retain much of my muscle mass, was able to care for myself, and was not experiencing many of the symptoms of someone having liver failure, the hospital was holding out for me to receive a really good liver. For a fleeting moment, I thought, "Finally! All that running and lifting weights paid off." I reveled in the fact that I was able to stave off the transplant for five weeks longer than the hospital had estimated because of the hard work I had put into staying strong and fit. I felt a sense of accomplishment at that moment, when I hadn't felt particularly good about anything.

The last thing I remember Dr. Frank saying to me was, "I don't want you to worry about anything. We are just waiting for a high quality liver to come in. Trust me, you are never further away from me than here." as he pointed to his heart. I thought that was weird and felt awkward, when all of a sudden he pulled a white piece of paper out of his even whiter doctor coat with a list of what he said was, "...a list of patients in need of a transplant." Thinking he had pointed to his heart, I felt like an idiot. I said, "I appreciate that, Dr. Frank; just don't wait too long." With that, Dr. Frank shook my hand and left.

Sue and I finished dinner then confirmed the plans for Saturday—I would wait to hear if I was having the test, after which time the doctors could more thoroughly evaluate my condition. Sue would stay with Aunt Marg at the convent and then come by as soon as visiting hours began again at 11:00 a.m. She kissed me, and told me that she loved me. I told her I loved her too, and after a supportive and warming embrace that I didn't want to end, we separated and she left.

That night, I lay in bed with my eyes wide open. I was beyond the state of being tired, but thoughts cycled continuously through my mind, and I was utterly unable to sleep. Thursday night into Friday morning had been the most excruciating ten hours of my life. The pain I had experienced was indescribable; it was beyond the limitations of language. I was shocked that the human body could take such a beating and survive. Although I was happy that staying in good shape had swung conditions in my favor, I wondered how much longer I would be able to hold out for a transplant. I could not escape the feeling inside that I had somehow dodged a bullet that day, but that at any moment that same bullet would swing around like a boomerang and hit me—no matter what I did to avoid it.

While lying on my left side, I gazed out into the hallway, and thought it was unusually quiet and unusually dark on the hospital floor. I felt as though I was at one end of a tunnel and could see light at the other end. Disturbed by that thought, I closed my eyes and turned over. I didn't want to sleep, knowing I was close to dying—I could feel it instinctively, but wasn't sure just how close. I wanted to live; I fought hard to live; and I thought that was enough to live. However, I knew that not everyone on the transplant waiting list lives long enough to get an organ, so I wondered if I too, would fall into that category. The emotions of the day were finally too much, and I fell asleep.

I was awakened the following morning at 5:30 a.m. by Dr. Burke's resident, Dr. Kennedy. I had seen him just the night before at 7:00 p.m. I noticed he was wearing a different shirt and tie, so I figured he must have gone home at some point. It turned out that he had caught a few hours of sleep at the hospital, showered, and returned to doing rounds. I felt sympathetic for the life of a resident doctor.

Dr. Kennedy asked me some questions about how I felt in general while checking my abdomen for unusual tenderness. As I conversed with Dr. Kennedy, another doctor walked in and silently sat down on the far side of the room. I had no idea who this doctor was, and his silence was disconcerting. I got the impression that Dr. Kennedy also did not know him.

After completing his examination, Dr. Kennedy explained that I would be undergoing the test that Dr. Burke had explained to me on Friday. It was then that the other doctor in the room spoke up, telling Dr. Kennedy to cancel the test since I was going for surgery. He then turned to me and said, "Mr. Bonner, my name is Dr. Markmann and I am one of the transplant surgeons. A liver has become available so we are going to bring you down for surgery. However, we have to go right now."

Chapter 2:
Never Forgotten

MY LIFE CHANGED DRAMATICALLY one Sunday afternoon when I was six years old. I know it was a Sunday because it was Easter Sunday and we were all dressed in our Easter best. Daddy had taken Ownie, me, and my younger sister, Bridget to the playground, while my Mom stayed behind with my youngest sister, Megan, who was only five months old at the time.

While playing on the monkey bars, I fell face first to the ground after losing my grip on one of the bars. I ended up with a bloodied nose and scraped knees, quickly running over to Daddy in need of something to wipe my nose and stop the bleeding. Daddy, dressed in a suit, had no tissues for me to use. Without hesitation, he ripped his suit pants pocket out so I could use that as a tissue. In my mind, he completely ruined his pants for me and with that, I began crying hysterically. I wished I had never fallen off the monkey bars; I wished my nose had never started bleeding and I certainly wished that Daddy had not ruined his pants for my sake.

From that day forward, I was a different person. When Daddy ruined his pants for me, he may as well have stepped in front of a bus for me. His was a level of self-sacrifice that I had seen only in movies before, but never understood. I understood right there on the playground that there are people, like my Dad, who are willing to sacrifice themselves for the good of others. With how badly I felt about being the beneficiary of such a sacrifice, my intention was to never again be the beneficiary; I wanted to be the one who sacrificed for others, just like my Dad.

My first real opportunity came two-and-a-half years later on Christmas Eve. I was playing football in the street with my friends when all of a sudden, a police car and ambulance came screaming up the street and planted themselves in front of our house. My heart pounded in my chest and my feet felt like anvils cemented to the ground as I watched several people rush inside. It was quiet for a few moments until the front door swung open, people jumped into the back of the ambulance and one person handed off something wrapped in a blanket to another person already in the ambulance. I stood by helplessly not knowing what happened as the ambulance sped away from our house. I later found out that the "something" was my sister, Megan. She had been watching me play football from the window, lost her balance, and fell palms-down on the searing-hot radiator. Her hands were completed bandaged, the covering of third-degree burns that spanned from her wrists to her fingertips on both hands.

The next morning as my family sat and opened presents, Megan's bandaged hands glided over the wrapping paper as if it were covered in grease. Heartbroken, I watched as my parents helped Megan tear the paper to reveal the new and shiny gift inside, only for her glee to turn to despair as she realized she could not play with anything she was given that

Christmas morning. Tears fell from our faces as I watched Megan's disappointment and frustration grow as each gift was opened. I did the only thing I could think of, and putting my presents aside, played with Megan for as long as she wanted with all the toys of her choice. I carried her dolls for her, fed them, and changed their diapers—whatever Megan wanted. My goal was to provide a means for Megan to share in the same Christmas joy as the rest of us despite what had happened to her hands.

When I went to bed that night, I never once thought about my own gifts. Playing with Megan all day had made me happier than any gift I could have gotten from Santa Claus. I shared more laughs with my sister that day than any other day I could recall in recent memory. For the first time in my life, I had done something selfless for another and never once wondered, "What's in it for me?" The incredible personal satisfaction I felt that day had me believing I was born to help others and that's what I wanted to do.

When I was 13, I found out that my "cousin," John, was sick. John was the eldest son of our neighbors, the Sciarabbas, whom we met while my family lived in Toms River, New Jersey, from 1973 to 1977. The Sciarabbas, Pete and Joann, had four kids, John, Mary Jo, Amy and Peter. Our families became extremely close, stayed in touch over the years, and became more like family than friends.

As always, I was ready to spring into action to help John when my parents told us he was sick but they had to break the news to us gently as John was more than just "sick." At first, John had digestive problems that became progressively worse. He endured the constant rotation of being in and out of hospitals, took various medications daily, and saw doctor after doctor in the hopes of getting better.

Over the years, John's digestive problems never improved. There was talk of him possibly needing to have surgery and wearing a colostomy bag for the rest of his life. John had also contracted a liver disease such that he was in need of a liver transplant. John eventually had the transplant, endured a twenty-hour surgery, and spent 30 days in the hospital recovering. As a 13-year-old kid, hearing things like digestive problems, colostomy bags, and liver transplants was more than I could comprehend. The way it translated in my mind was that John was sick and it was serious.

My family was invited to a benefit concert shortly after we moved to Bayville, NJ in 1986 to help raise money for John's swelling medical bills. That night, as I sat in the audience listening to numerous singers take the stage, I felt that I was part of something special. The community rallied behind John, someone about whom I cared very deeply, to make a contribution and help alleviate the financial burden that weighed the whole family down. I remember feeling very proud that I knew John, and proud to be sitting there on his behalf. I just wished *I* could do something meaningful to help him. John certainly had no dolls for me to carry around, nor could I buy him a pair of pants to fix the situation he faced. I was, however, determined to find something, anything, I could do for him. I even asked God to take away the pain that John had and give it to me; maybe then John could get the break he deserved.

John was well enough to work in house construction in the summer of 1987. Being drawn to John because of his problems, and wanting to help him in some way, I offered to do odd jobs at the construction site. I stacked wood, got food and drinks for the crew—whatever John needed. On days when the work was finished early, we picked up Ownie (my older brother) and went to play "home run derby" at the local park. John had played baseball in high school and was eager to see how he fared after his transplant. The rules of home run derby were simple: you hit a home run, you got a point; the person with the most points at the end of the game was the winner. OB and I played home run derby with John several times that summer, though John never did hit a home run. His lack of strength and stamina were obvious. Nevertheless, John always went out there, swung his hardest, and tried to get a point up on the board. While I played the outfield watching Ownie pitch and John hit, often I became overwhelmed with sadness as I wanted John to get a home run probably more than he did. Even without a home run, it was great to see John healthy again and enjoying himself.

While I was a sophomore in college, I received news that John was in need of a second liver transplant, about ten years after his original transplant. I have very few details of John's second transplant, other than the fact that he needed one and that he got one. Due to improvements in medicine, the surgery wasn't as long as the first, nor was the length of his hospital stay. John fully recovered after the second transplant and was doing well.

Early in the spring semester of my junior year, my parents called to tell me that John was in the hospital. I asked why, and they told me that he suffered a fall from his dirt bike. While in the hospital, John began to have complications – complications of what, and how severe, I wasn't sure. My mother called me a few days later to tell me that John had passed away. He was only 29.

To say that I was devastated is rather an underestimation of the conglomerate of feelings I had—not only of grief for his passing but the inescapable feeling that I had never done anything meaningful for him, and now he was gone. Sadness filled every possible square inch of my body in that instant—the moment my mother said that John had left us. My mind flashed back to memories of working with John during the summer and playing home run derby. I thought about how inspirational he was, and how I so wanted to help him and couldn't. I simply could not bring myself to grapple with the cold fact that he died, despite the fact that he had never done anything to deserve the fate he was given. All I could do was hope - hope and pray - that he died peacefully and without pain. Anger and frustration soon poured from my ears as though I was an erupting volcano and I soon found that I was brimming with fury.

"Why! Why! Why?" was all I could bring myself to think. I stared up, straining my eyes as if I could see God through the ceiling. I was raised as a Catholic, was a strong believer in God, and had always felt a closeness to God. However, at that moment, I was angry with God, and I wanted God to know that I was angry with Him. I wanted to know why John was never cut a break, why he had to go through what he did, and why God never seemed to do anything to save him. I even told God he could have given whatever John had to me and I would have been totally fine with that. I knew the clouds weren't going to open up, nor was God going to appear and give me the answers I wanted, but it didn't stop me from wanting Him to just the same. It took me a while to calm down, and when I did, nothing changed. John was gone. There wasn't anything I could do about it.

Another tidal wave of sadness crashed over me as I thought about Uncle Pete, Aunt Joann, and the rest of the Sciarabba family. I couldn't begin to imagine how heartbroken they must have been. I so longed to hug and tell them all that it would be all right, but the reality was that even if I could reach out to touch them, nothing was going to change this moment. Not now. Not ever. Life for Uncle Pete and Aunt Joann had changed forever. Just as I had wanted John's pain to be taken from him when he was alive, I now wanted Uncle Pete and Aunt Joann's pain whisked away along with Mary Jo, Amy and Peter's. Not even God could have granted such a wish.

John's wake and funeral were held in Mississippi. Aunt Joann was originally from there and later the family relocated. To this day, I'm not sure why, but no one from my family attended the services. I have never felt comfortable with this, given the fact that we were so close with the Sciarabbas. I wanted the entire family to know that I loved them all, and was holding them close to my heart. Ironically,

I don't ever recall ever speaking to Uncle Pete, Aunt Joann, Mary Jo, Amy, or Peter to express my condolences. I guess, in retrospect, that I was too afraid of what I would or wouldn't say that could possibly make them feel more grief than they already did.

John passed away in February, 1994, and I miss him to this day. After talking with Mary Jo, Amy, and Peter about John's passing, it came to light that one of his biggest concerns was not dying, but that he would be forgotten. No one can ever take away the fond memories I have of John as they are with me always. I guarantee that for as long as I am alive, he will never be forgotten.

I struggled constantly with my emotions after John's death, feeling that it never should have happened and that he should still be alive. Aggravated and dismayed, I was unsure of what to think and how to feel. I wanted God to know exactly how I felt, but could never bring myself to tell Him the depths of my disappointment and frustration. How does one tell the being whom you believe to have created the heavens and the earth that you are disappointed with Him and feel like there was some sort of mistake? I just couldn't do it. Overwhelmed with sorrow and unable to rationalize John's death in any meaningful way, I needed a break from God. There was so much confusion in my head and I just didn't know where God fit in with all of it. I had become hardened and incapable at that time of forgiving God for what happened to John, as though it were His fault. I had asked many times to be given whatever John had, so he could finally have a break. I had trusted God to do the right thing, and I was let down. Since my requests to help John fell on deaf ears time and time again, I finally decided I no longer wanted anything to do with God; and I no longer wanted God to have anything to do with me. Thankfully, God was not as quick to turn his back on me as I was on Him.

Chapter 3:
So It Begins

ON MONDAY, APRIL 15, 1996, after working through my lunch, I heard and felt something from deep inside my stomach that I never before experienced. My stomach gave a loud grumbling noise as if it were a violent hunger pang, followed by what is best described as my stomach falling and landing, hard, somewhere just above my groin. I tried to figure out what it could have been, when my body screamed at me to get to a bathroom and get there N-O-W! I jumped up from my seat and took off.

As I ran to the bathroom, I unbuckled my belt and pants before I got to the men's room, for fear that I wasn't going to make it in time. I got to the men's room, threw open the door, got into the first stall, and pulled my pants down as fast as humanly possible. There was no time to cover the seat with the protective tissue paper seat cover. As soon as I hit the seat, an explosion came out of my body, the strength of which nearly caused me to lose consciousness. Frantically, I pressed my hands against either side of the stall and struggled to keep from passing out. I broke out in a cold sweat that quickly drenched my head and face. A tingling sensation traveled through my hands, giving me the familiar feeling of "pins and needles" when your hands fall asleep. There were several waves of stomach cramping then expulsion followed by more stomach cramping and expulsion. I had no idea what was happening or why.

There was a sharp pain in my stomach that felt as though I had been impaled and the sword left there stabbing into my gut. The pain stayed with me even after the explosions had ceased, leaving my body cavity feeling utterly empty and destroyed. I gathered some toilet paper and proceeded to clean myself, when I saw, much to my disgust and horror, that the toilet paper was covered in blood. I stood and stared into the toilet at what looked like a vicious murder scene. The blood was everywhere, leaving not a single trace of what would accompany a normal bowel movement. It was bright red, as though it had been pumped freshly out of my veins, and splattered over the entire inside of the toilet changing the water to a murky scarlet color. I stood there in pain, confused, disheartened, and revolted. It took several wads of toilet paper to completely clean myself and numerous flushes to force the toilet paper down. I was sure not to leave any traces of blood behind, so the next person in the bathroom wouldn't witness the same horror I did.

As I washed my hands and face in the sink, sweat continued to pour from my body as though I had just run a marathon. I took some paper towels, soaked them in cold water and placed them on the back of my neck. The cooling sensation of the cloth felt comforting on my neck and my body began the process of balancing itself. I stood silently for a few moments as the sweating stopped and the shaking in my hands and legs subsided to a tremble. I left that restroom a broken man. Incredibly weak and excruciatingly thirsty, I stopped at the water fountain on the way back to my desk. By this time the physical pain was overtaken by the humiliation I felt. I had no idea what the hell had just happened. All I knew was that I wanted to go home and boil myself to rid my brain and my body of that afternoon. I had never felt so dehumanized before in all my life at the utter lack of control over my physical body.

I left work that night concerned about the episode in the bathroom, but rationalized that it must have been something I'd eaten that day. After skipping dinner and watching some TV with my roommates, I went to bed. My stomach rumbled as though I had eaten something that was now eating me from the inside. I had no idea what could be happening since there was nothing in my digestive system.

I woke the next morning and began ironing a shirt for work. There was no rumbling, but within minutes of ironing the shirt, I again had another emergency situation and ran down the stairs, desperately trying to make it to the bathroom in time. It felt like my insides were pouring out as I clenched my stomach and gasped at my loss of breath. There was no blood, this time, only a bowel movement that highly resembled a bowl of oatmeal. My hands and legs shook violently once again and I felt very weak. Once I had gathered myself, I cleaned up, got some juice from the refrigerator, and went upstairs to take a shower. It was apparent that my stomach "issue" was not an isolated incident, but perhaps a stomach virus of some sort that was wreaking havoc on my body.

I avoided food all day Tuesday except for a peanut

butter and jelly sandwich Tuesday night. Feeling slightly better Wednesday, I tried eating a turkey and cheese sandwich, though unfortunately it tasted like worms. I forced it down, since I hadn't eaten barely a thing over the last few days but still finished only one half and threw the other half in the garbage. I was surprised by my lack of appetite but figured it was a side effect of the stomach bug that I was carrying around. Within an hour of returning to the office, I was in the bathroom having another episode. There were no traces of blood but more oatmeal-like diarrhea. I was thankful there was no blood but concerned that I was still unwell. Never wanting to go to a doctor, I waited to see how my condition would progress.

Over the next several weeks, I had repeated bouts of diarrhea, bloody diarrhea, low-grade fevers, stomach pain, and nausea. Despite this, it seemed that my condition never really worsened and even showed some signs of improvement, so I never went to see a doctor.

My emotional condition, though, was a different story. I began to develop a hatred toward food because of how my body reacted shortly thereafter. As a result, I drastically changed my eating habits: I ate a small breakfast, small lunch, and a light dinner. I also dreaded getting ready for work in the morning, since the past few weeks had shown that to be the worst time of day. I would sometimes need to use the bathroom two or three times in an hour before finally leaving the house for work. Going through this routine on a daily basis had begun to drag me down into a deep depression. I often stayed confined in the house, afraid that if I left, there would be another public bathroom incident. I also avoided family and friends, not wanting to suffer the indignity of telling them what had been happening to me. I was a hot-head to begin with, but the unknown condition really had me agitated, almost every waking minute, of every day.

To assuage some of the emotional stress, I began to drink alcohol more than usual. My roommates and I turned Thursday nights into a junk-food-eating, video-game-playing-and-drinking extravaganza. My drink of choice soon became gin martinis, specifically, Tanqueray martinis. At first, I struggled to drink a martini since it was nothing but alcohol. I ended up devouring an entire sleeve of crackers to kill the taste of the gin. The crackers would, in turn, dry my mouth and I would need another drink. It was the perfect cycle of sip, cracker, sip, cracker, until both the martini and sleeve of crackers were gone. When my roommates prepared for Thursday nights, they would always have a sleeve of crackers ready for me. It wasn't long before I didn't need the crackers anymore, as the martinis went down much easier all on their own.

Thursday nights became an emotional crutch for me; it was the only time during the week that I could eat what I want, drink what I want, and have fun, since I was comfortable inside my house. Any other time I was outside the house, even just to go to work, an outburst could occur at any time without warning. Resenting the fact that my life had been reduced to such a state I became irritable, defensive, and callous to my family, friends, and co-workers.

I am amazed that any of these people tolerated me during that time.

Alcohol had varying affects on me when I drank. For whatever reason, a really cold beer would substantially ease the pain in my stomach. There were other times when drinking a beer felt like razor blades slicing through my body. To compensate for the potential problems from drinking, I changed my habits to facilitate the least amount of pain and digestive anguish. I drank faster, hoping that getting buzzed would diminish any pain I might feel, and I drank less beer and more hard alcohol. I got buzzed faster and didn't have to drink as much. For me, it was a win-win situation, or so I thought. Any time you rationally believe that drinking faster, drinking more, or drinking hard alcohol will fix your problems, you probably have some misfiring synapses in your brain. I was desperate for a fix to my problem, and alcohol was cheap, easy, and did the trick most of the time.

I was truly desperate for answers but refused to go to see a doctor. The symptoms all involved parts of my body I wasn't comfortable with, so I sure as hell was not comfortable having to A) explain what was happening to someone else and B) having that person examine those body parts—no way. This meant that the only place left was the internet.

I found a website with a form into which you could enter your symptoms, answer some basic questions, and get a list of possible diseases or conditions that match those symptoms. As I typed in my information: diarrhea, bloody diarrhea, stomach pain, unexpected weight loss, occasional fever, weakness, loss of appetite, etc., I became apprehensive about revealing the possible "matches" for my symptoms. I kept thinking, "Please don't be cancer. Please don't be cancer."

When I hit the "enter" button, I was stunned by the results: AIDS. AIDS?? What do you mean, AIDS? There was no way I had AIDS – absolutely not. I had never used drugs and I was sexually responsible. I just couldn't conceive that this was a possibility. In that instant, I was furious, demoralized and ashamed. I thought to myself, "I am a better person than this and I could have prevented it. I don't deserve this, God damn it!"

That's when it hit me: GOD. Could it be that God was trying to get my attention? Could it be that God was finally getting around to all my requests to help John, by taking his pain away and giving it to me, though it was way too late? In my despondency, I felt it was definitely possible. If I had solved the case and that's what was happening here, why now? What good could it do? Now that I was in pain, I wasn't so sure I wanted to take away someone else's pain after all.

Paranoid as to why God was doing this to me, I thought that perhaps He was trying to teach me a lesson for turning my back on Him. One thing was certain: I had to know if I really did have AIDS. I ordered an AIDS in-home testing kit to be delivered. I refused to be tested anywhere other than in the privacy of my own home where I could call a number a few days later to get the results. I followed the directions in the kit when it arrived and mailed the test out immediately. It would be at least three or four days before I got the results. I couldn't concentrate on anything; I didn't want to be at work; and I didn't want to talk to anyone. I wanted to be left alone, even retreating from my roommates, my family, and my friends. I was living in a personal hell and I just wanted it to be over.

I called the number from the testing kit the moment my results were available. My hands shook and my heart raced as the recorded voice told me to enter my code number and press the pound key. After I entered the code the recording said, "One moment, please," then returned and said quite stoically, "Your test results are negative." I repeated the recording a few more times just to be sure I had heard correctly – my results were negative. Even though I had been off God for more than two years, I took a moment of thanks for not putting this on me. It was hypocritical, since I had asked God to give me John's pain and didn't feel I had the right to pick or choose what I should or shouldn't receive to balance things out. If God decided I should get AIDS, then I'd have to deal with that.

After my temporary elation passed, I became extremely frightened. With one possibility eliminated, the door still stood wide open for the true offender to be cancer or some other terrifying disease. The weeks of continuous stress had taken their toll on me and I emotionally imploded. It was time to see a doctor.

Chapter 4:
Peanut Butter Swirls

BEFORE GOING TO THE DOCTOR, I had to talk to my roommates, Jon and Jay. They were my partners in crime for Thursday night drinks, bad eating, and video games. I figured it would be easier to talk to both of them at the same time, since an emergency bathroom episode could strike at any given moment and I would need access to the toilet with almost no notice.

I had hoped that by telling Jon, he would call his father for me, who was an internist, and somehow magically receive terrific news. Jon did call his dad, who felt it would be best that I see a doctor and have a rectal exam. I feared this would be the case and tried putting the moment on hold for as long as possible but understood I couldn't avoid it any longer. My one-way street was about to become a two-way street, much to my disappointment.

Sensing that I wasn't happy with what Jon's father suggested, both Jon and Jay began to try and lighten the situation. Some of the more memorable quotes from that evening included, "Damn, brother. The doctor is going to get all Captain Stinkfinger on you." "He's going to have to get all up in there." and "The doctor is going to go spelunking in your cave." I laughed with them, especially after the spelunking comment as "Spelunker" became my new nickname, but wasn't laughing after they went to bed. I couldn't sleep. The thought of having someone invade my body in that way preoccupied my thoughts and I was restless.

A new wave of depression came over me. More than anything in the world, I did not want to have a rectal exam. That area of my body was off-limits to everyone, including me. The thought of now having it examined by a stranger made my head spin. I even began to have second thoughts about my mystery illness entirely, thinking that maybe I had over-inflated the severity of the situation. The truth I had tried desperately to avoid was that I was already six months into going to the bathroom eight-to-ten times daily, with blood now accompanying every bowel movement. I had to see a doctor but first had to find the courage to endure the examination. While trying to find my courage, I lost more weight from not wanting to eat anything at all. I felt lethargic most of the time, and had no desire to go to work, the gym, or associate with friends. My life had been reduced to staying home and shutting out the rest of the world.

Going to bed at night was the worst. It was when, as I would say, the demons came to get me. The "demons" were the product of my all-consuming anxiety. I closed my eyes to try and fall asleep quickly but never could. My brain would spin chaotically into a million directions, all filled with anguish over what could possibly be wrong with me and what tests I might have to endure. Most of all, I anguished over what the bathroom situation would be the next morning.

For about six weeks prior to making the dreaded doctor's appointment, my morning routine was like clockwork: I woke up, went to the bathroom five or six times, each time splattering blood all over the toilet, endured sharp pains in my stomach, took a shower, ironed a shirt, skipped breakfast, and left the house. It became so routine one could set a watch to it. It was at the end of those six weeks that I finally decided I couldn't take it anymore.

Since I had never really been sick before, I had to figure out how my health insurance worked when trying to locate a doctor. It turned out I had to see a primary care physician in the network of my HMO insurance plan to conduct an initial examination. I found one close to my house, gave the receptionist my information, and scheduled the appointment.

When I arrived at the office, I had to fill out the usual paperwork with my personal information and my insurance data. There was a small section wherein I was to write down the symptoms I was experiencing. It was then that I froze, unable to fit into this little box the story of my life for the past half-year. Still, the pen continued writing and as I wrote, I felt that the people in the waiting room knew exactly what I had said and were looking at me in disgust. I handed the paperwork to the receptionist and stood there as she read what I just wrote. In a well-rehearsed comfort-voice, she said, "Ok. Have a seat and the doctor will be right with you."

The doctor arrived shortly and asked me to explain what was wrong. I thought, "C'mon – just read the paperwork I filled out." I paused for a moment trying to find the right words to say and began my explanation in a whisper hoping that no one else would hear me talk about bloody diarrhea and stomach pain. I then explained how many times I went to the bathroom throughout the day, the pain I had, the weight loss, blah, blah, blah. I began to hope the doctor would say, "Just take this medication, and you'll be fine." but that's obviously not what happened.

After the doctor listened to my story, he said, "Ok, let me check you out." I froze. When he picked up the blood pressure cuff, I took a much-needed breath. The doctor took my blood pressure, listened to my heart, checked my eyes and my throat, and then said, "Everything looks ok." I felt instantly as if the 1,000 pound weight I had been carrying around all day simply fell away. Then it happened, suddenly and without warning: "I'm going to have to check your rectum for traces of blood." Seizing any available opportunity to discredit the need for the rectal exam, I thought, "Wait a second. There is no reason for you to check my rectum for traces of blood. I am telling you that there *are* traces of blood. Why would I make that up? DO YOU THINK I WANT YOU TO STICK SOMETHING IN THERE??"

Since it didn't seem that raging paranoia was the best possible venue to pursue, I asked the doctor very calmly despite the screaming in my head, "Is that really necessary?" The doctor then said rather flatly, "Yes. I want to test the concentration of blood that is present." Again, even more reluctantly, I said, "Ok, what do you need me to do?" He then proceeded to walk over to the counter, where he had a full box of pre-powdered examination gloves and a large tube of KY Jelly. He said, "Pull your pants down and lie on your left side."

Having to pull my pants down and lie on my side was by far the most degrading moment of my life. I hated being naked in front of anyone that wasn't female, and I wasn't terribly comfortable then either. I hated being naked in front of other guys so much so that I never showered in the gym. Lying naked on a table in front of a doctor was new territory for me. I wanted to be anywhere but there at that very moment. I tried to mentally block out what was about to happen by looking for some pattern on the wall that would remind me of puppies, clouds, fish, or anything other than a foreign object about to be placed in my rectum. My entire body was tense as the doctor walked toward me. He said, "Lift your knees to your chest. Good. Now you are going to feel some pressure." I didn't want to feel pressure. I didn't want to feel anything. I didn't want to be there. I didn't want to be sick. I didn't want any of this.

I felt what seemed to be something the size of a soda can forced into my rectum. Either this guy duped me into thinking he was going to use his finger and actuality put something else far larger in there, or he had the biggest man-hands on the planet. I felt him swirl his finger around as if he were trying to scrape the bottom of the peanut jar for that last bit of butter. After several uncomfortable swishes and swirls, he removed his inhumanly large finger without warning. I continued to lie there breathing through my mouth as the doctor said, "Ok, you can get dressed."

That was the precursor to my final moment of humiliation for the day. As the doctor was waiting for the results of the test, he handed me some tissues with which to wipe myself. I felt like I was his prison bitch and had to clean myself up after he'd had his way with me. I felt incredibly violated and wanted to go home and scrub away all the skin on my body. Shortly thereafter, the doctor again rather flatly said, "It looks like you have a large concentration of blood in your stool." I avoided the strong temptation to say, "No shit, Sherlock." He then explained to me that he couldn't diagnose me and would have to refer me to a specialist for further testing. Great—all that for nothing.

The doctor gave me a referral to a local gastroenterologist. At that time I didn't know what gastroenterologists specialized in, and didn't particularly care. I was content knowing I would be seeing someone who studied digestive health and disorders. When I left the office, I had only a paltry amount of pride compared to when I first arrived. Still, I sat in my car for a moment hoping the worst was behind me. I was one step closer to finding out what was wrong, and in that moment, that thought provided enough incentive for me to gather myself together and get on with it – next stop, an appointment with a gastro.

When I met the gastro for the first time, he was small in stature and had an uneasy air about him as though he didn't want to be there. I couldn't blame him. Sticking my finger into strange people's anuses is not a career path I would have chosen. However, being that this was his chosen career path, the least he could have done was try to make people in uncomfortable situations like mine feel more comfortable.

The doctor and I exchanged greetings and got down to business. I explained my symptoms, how long they had been occurring, and what the primary care physician had said. The words flowed a little easier this time, after growing past the initial experience. He said, "Ok, let's run some tests. I'll have to check the concentration of blood in your rectum." I thought to myself, "When are these guys just going to take my word for it and do something other than stick something in my ass?" But rather than racing thoughts, paranoia or extreme anxiety, I simply proceeded to unbutton my pants and lie on my left side. Once again I began searching for bunnies and other pleasantries in the wallpaper that would temporarily distract me from the invasion. I heard the typical, "You're going to feel some pressure" comment followed by that illusive finger. After the initial "pressure," I felt the old familiar peanut-butter swirl a few times, and then an abrupt exit. The doctor said, "It appears there is a large concentration of blood in your rectum." I sighed.

He then offered to talk more with me in his office once I had finished cleaning up. I felt a twinge of concern shoot up my spine, since the only images I had of doctor consultations were from movies, when someone was usually given extremely bad news. I went into the office thinking the worst and prepared to listen for words like HIV/AIDS, cancer, tumor, or fatal. As a digestive disorder novice, these were the only words on my radar screen.

I sat in a nice leather chair in front of a very large, beautiful, wooden desk. The doctor sat behind the desk and looked even more uncomfortable than he did before. This made me even more uncomfortable since I knew he was uncomfortable. The doctor said he wanted me to have some blood drawn for testing, a stool sample for testing, and a colonoscopy. Once he received the results from these tests, he felt that he would be able to give me an accurate diagnosis and begin treating me. Due to the severity of the symptoms, he asked me to act quickly to minimize my discomfort. I didn't hear any of the words I was keying in on (HIV/AIDS, cancer, tumor, fatal) so I was confused and required clarification. I started firing questions in short, rapid succession:

Me: "Is it cancer?"

Doctor: "No."

Me: "Is it a tumor?"

Doctor: "No. Highly unlikely." (No was all I really cared about anyway)

Me: "Could this be something fatal?"

Doctor: "Not necessarily."

Me: "What do you mean?"

Doctor: "I'll need to get test results back but I highly doubt it's anything fatal."

Me: "But it could be?"

Doctor: "Most likely not."

Me: "Could it be HIV or AIDS? I put my symptoms in on the internet and that's what it told me I could have. I took a test at home but it came out negative."

Doctor: "Then I'm sure it's negative. I will be able to tell you more when I get your test results."

Me: "Ok. What's a colonoscopy?"

Doctor: "It's a test where I place a special tube equipped with a camera into your rectum and inspect the inside of your colon."

Me: "Is that really necessary?" (rising anxiety)

Doctor: "The results from your blood work along with your colonoscopy will tell me exactly what's going on."

Me: "Is it painful?"

Doctor: "No. I will give you a sedative that will cause you to be semi-conscious. Chances are you won't remember anything. However, you will need someone to drive you home after the procedure and you should not return to work that day."

Me: "Ok. Is there anything else I should know? I mean, is there anything else that you may not be telling me because you think I can't handle it?"

Doctor: "No. We need to take this one step at a time so let's get some of these tests out of the way and schedule an office visit after the colonoscopy. You can set up a time to have the colonoscopy with my assistant."

While the conversation was as awkward as it sounds, I couldn't think of any other questions to ask at that point, so I agreed to his instructions, shook his hand, thanked him for his time, and to went off to schedule with the assistant. I was given a prescription for blood work, a prescription for a stool sample packet and scheduled the colonoscopy for two weeks later.

I left the doctor's office and headed to the nearest lab to have the blood samples taken. While there, I was also able to pick up supplies for the stool sample. The packet included several plastic pill bottles, a printout of directions, and a small scooper. I realized I would have to wait until I got home to figure out just how all of this was going to work.

Once I was home, I read the directions carefully on how to obtain a good stool sample. The directions included phrases such as: "The sample must not get wet," "Use the scooper to transfer the sample to the bottle," and "Keep the sample refrigerated until drop off." What? How am I going to keep this dry? Do they expect me to go to the bathroom in the tub, transfer it, and then clean it up? That doesn't sound right. Maybe they expect me to go to the bathroom on a plastic bag or something, transfer it, and then just throw the bag away? Nah. As I was running through different scenarios in my head, it became something of a mission impossible. I began to think of it as, "Operation Fecal Freak."

An engineer, I am not. Therefore, it became increasingly clear that I had to get creative and search the house for possible solutions and tools I might utilize. I found a cardboard box bottom under a case of beer and thought, "Perfect." It was relatively flat, could cover the circumference of the toilet bowl or most of it, was sturdy enough to hold a number two, provided easy access to a number two, and could be easily discarded. What else could one ask for when transferring one's stool to a pill bottle?

I inspected the box bottom further to ensure it could stand up to the challenge. Upon further inspection, my only concern was that the box bottom could be extremely dirty and I didn't want to take the chance of contaminating my sample. I came up with a simple solution: I would place a garbage bag over the top of the box bottom. That way, I could prevent the sample from being contaminated and could easily fold the bag over the box bottom and throw it away. I put my concoction in the upstairs bathroom, proud of my ingenuity, and waited for a number two.

As soon as I had a number two in the on-deck circle ready to make its major league debut, I went upstairs, took the lid off of the pill bottles and made sure the scooper was in arm's reach. Next, I lifted the lid on the toilet seat and placed the box bottom across the top of the bowl. I placed the garbage bag over the box bottom and put the seat down. I then proceeded to remove my sneakers, pants and underwear just in case some disaster occurred, although I had no idea what that disaster might entail. I then used the sink counter to balance myself, hovered over the toilet, and took care of business. When I was finished, I took the box bottom off the toilet, cleaned myself, and put the box bottom back on the toilet.

I took a moment to inspect what was now sitting in a heap before me. It looked more like my recent bowel movements so I thought it would be a good sample. I grabbed the scooper and the pill bottles and got down to business. My tactic was simple: just scoop off the top, try not to look at it, and get it in the pill bottle as quickly and cleanly as possible. Trying not to smell it was impossible, and it wasn't long before the stench filled the bathroom even though the fan was cranking at top speed. There was a "fill line" on each bottle that indicated how much of the bottle should be filled with stool, so I just scooped and filled, scooped and filled. At one point, I came across something I couldn't quite identify so I put that in there as well. After completing the task, I folded up the garbage bag, put it into another garbage bag, and brought it outside. Operation Fecal Freak was a success.

Word had begun to spread around this time within my family and circle of friends that something was wrong with me and I had to undergo testing. I joked, when they asked, about having to land a stool sample and the means by which I acquired one. Joking about the situation was my way of downplaying what I was going through, and how I truly felt about it all. I didn't want other people to know just how lowly and degraded I felt.

If anyone had discovered at the time what I was truly feeling they would have been shocked at its comparison to the façade I showed others. I had thoughts that I called non-suicidal suicidal, meaning that I wanted to die but didn't want to take my own life. What would my family and friends think hearing that? How could they possibly react to something like, "After my exam, I want to go home and scrub the skin off my body." They would have been tremendously frightened. But, this was truly how I felt, and I was a prisoner to my feelings.

With the colonoscopy looming on the horizon, my anxiety level rose to an all-time high. There was no way I could brave this one alone and there was only one person in the entire world that I trusted enough to go through it with me: my Dad. I knew I had to break down, call him, and tell him really what was going on, joking aside.

Chapter 5:
The Constant

BEFORE I LEFT FOR college, I had a conversation with Daddy, who said that if he ever had to walk through the fires of hell, he would choose me to go with him. I told him that I felt the same about him. Mentally and physically preparing myself for a colonoscopy was my equivalent of walking through the fires of hell, so I gave Daddy a call.

In an effort to ensure a level of privacy, I called him at work since I knew he could talk without any third party overhearing the conversation. Keeping the colonoscopy as private as possible, even from my own family, was of paramount importance to me. I felt that the more people knew, the more they would ask questions, and the more attention would be directed toward me and my condition. I was absolutely determined to keep things on the down-low.

When Dad picked up the phone, he answered in his business voice, "Owen Bonner, can I help you?" I said, "Hey, what's going on?" and he replied, "Hey, Guy, what's up?" Daddy used to call me "Guy" or "Big Guy" when I called him at the office. "Not much. I need to ask a favor." "Shoot," he said. "The doctor wants me to have a test done and I need someone go with me." Without letting me explain further, without hesitation, and without reservation, Daddy simply stated, "I'm there." "Ok, thanks." I said. "I'll fill you in on the details later." and quickly hung up the phone. At the moment I clicked the receiver, I broke down. My feelings at that point were ready to explode as I realized just how unsuccessfully I had struggled to deal with all of this alone. When Daddy said, "I'm there" every ounce of emotion that I had been packing away, trying not to feel, came gushing out and I could no longer control it. I hadn't even consciously realized how vulnerable I truly felt and how the fear surrounding my health had consumed me. I was desperate—desperate to feel the same love and safety I had felt as a child. His simple, quickly spoken words, "I'm there." filled the void and soothed my gaping wounds exquisitely as only my dad could do. It was like he ripped out his pants pocket for me all over again.

The day before the colonoscopy proved to be more interesting than I could ever have anticipated. I had to "prep" for 24 hours prior to the procedure, which included a fast of only chicken broth or any "non-red" Jell-o and clear liquids. In addition to the assorted liquids, I also had to drink the very tasty Fleet Phospho-Soda Oral Saline Laxative to promote bowel movements. Luckily for me, it came in lemon flavor; whatever lemon-flavored dog shit tastes like, that is.

Not knowing just what to expect, I decided to chance it and go to work that day. Now, I've learned as I grow older that there are moments in life that exist beyond the reach of linguistic description. The sounds and smells of that fine day stand as a monument to this simple, not-so-quiet truth. It was awful, especially combined with my longstanding aversion to public restrooms, in which I spent the great majority of the day. Once home that evening, I found myself awaiting the impending colonoscopy, since at least I would be only semi-conscious, which would temper the embarrassment surrounding this whole mess.

The next morning, Daddy arrived just before 7:30 a.m., which meant he had left his house between 5:30 a.m. and 6:00 a.m. We didn't talk much; I just gave him directions to the office. Daddy knew I didn't want to talk, so we simply didn't. I signed in once we were at the office, took a seat, and waited to be called. During that time we didn't speak much either. Only when they called my name for the procedure did Daddy give me a kiss and say, "Good luck. I'll be here when you get out."

Daddy was great. He knew I had a lot on my mind, so he gave me the space I wanted. He could see that I was concerned about the colonoscopy, so he gave me support at exactly the right moment. He was also intuitive and secure enough in our relationship that he never once tried to initiate the cliché father-son dissertation about how he loves me and will be there to hold my hand, or any of that crap I had no desire to hear. "I'll be here when you get out." It was short, sweet, and the only words that the moment required.

In retrospect, I had anticipated the colonoscopy to be far worse than it actually was. The nurse began an IV (intravenous injection) and wheeled me into a room on a gurney after which the doctor administered a sedative, and I woke up in recovery. I was not at all coherent during the procedure.

When I awoke, Daddy was there just as he said he would be. A nurse came in and gave me a half of a turkey sandwich and some apple juice. My throat was parched from the anesthesia and I'd had no solids in well over 24 hours, making it seem that this was the best-tasting lunch I'd ever eaten in my life. It was then that a curious dialogue ensued between Daddy and me:

Daddy asked, "How do you feel?" I said, "Fine. What'd the doctor say?"

Daddy went on to explain that the doctor thought the procedure went well and that I should make an appointment to follow-up with him in his office. I told Daddy that I had already scheduled a follow-up but wanted more details about what exactly the doctor   had said.

Confused as to what exactly I expected him to say, Daddy just said, "The doctor said everything was fine but nothing else." I pressed further as I had an insatiable desire to know word-for-word what was said so I could piece things together myself. "But what exactly did he say?"

Daddy, patient but on edge said, "All he told me was that the procedure was fine and that he would speak to you soon." I asked if I could talk to the doctor myself but Daddy said that he had left to see another patient. Apparently, I wasn't pleased with that answer and yelled out, "I don't give a shit where he is. You tell that mother-fucker to get his ass over here right now."

"Watch your mouth!" Daddy barked. "You can call his office later if you want." Very calmly I said, "Ok." and returned to eating my delicious turkey sandwich. After I was done with my sandwich, I turned to Daddy and asked, "So, did you talk to the doctor yet?" Daddy had no idea what was going on and simply said, "I already told you I talked with him and he said everything was fine."

I was not forewarned about the possible side-effects of the anesthesia, and I can only assume that my lack of control over my word choices fell into that category. At first waking I wasn't able to comprehend or retain any information, after which time I became belligerent, then simply wandered around mentally until falling asleep again. I must have been satisfied with my dad's final response to that conversation, since I don't remember much of anything after that. He later, good-naturedly, told me about the outburst. I apologized and then thanked him for all he had done for me that day, including his drive of over four hours just for one doctor's appointment. "Anytime." He said, and that was all the response that was needed.

My journey with chronic illness took me down a long and treacherous psychological path, one that vacillated between the darkest caverns of wretched self-pity and explosive anger to moments of edifying insight as I began to gain a greater understanding and appreciation of the suffering of others. Trust me when I say that having a stable support system in place is critical when walking this road. For me, that came in the form of my dad and my family.

Having my dad's support meant I didn't always have to put on a brave face—it removed the pressure to put on society's idealized mask of the masculine macho face—a façade that really does no one any substantial good. He listened when I would yell and swear after things didn't go well. He was there to offer a hand to hold when I needed affection. He was there when I was vulnerable and couldn't fend for myself. I cannot stress how important it is to have someone who can provide this level of support to you in your time of need. I tried it both ways—with the macho mask and later without—and I highly preferred the latter, because at least it was honest and truly human.

I don't know exactly when it was that Daddy acquired the nickname, but he loved to be referred to as "The Constant." I honestly don't know if I had assigned him that name, if our whole family had labeled him as such, or if Daddy gave himself the name. In any event, he enjoyed it. During any stressful situation he would say, "I'm The Constant," and place both hands together in front of him, palms facing down, and move them apart in a slow, steady, fluid motion. The four of us kids would laugh and say things like, "Get out of here." "Shut up, Dad!" or "Please!" Realistically, the entire family was extremely grateful. We were silently appreciative that Daddy truly was "The Constant," though we never personally admitted it to him. He was there, for each and every one of us, in such a complete and caring way. The Constant had a powerful, and tremendously positive, impact on us all.

It was February of 1997 when I drove to the gastroenterologist's office to consult with him about my colonoscopy results. I sat in the same leather chair, in front of the same beautiful wooden desk, and again, the doctor seemed to be uncomfortable with both the surroundings and the conversation we were about to have. He said in a forced, overly positive voice, "It appears from the results of your tests that you have a digestive disorder called ulcerative colitis (UC). I'll explain what that is..." Instead of trying to remember what was said verbatim, let me summarize:

UC is a disease that affects the intestines. Essentially, there are three types of UC, which I've come to designate as part, half, and whole; part of your intestines could be affected, half your intestines, or the whole intestine, with each level considered to be progressively more serious. As luck would have it, my whole intestine was affected. This was of particular importance in my case since although UC is not cancer, it greatly increases the risk of developing colon cancer for those who suffer from it. The risk of cancer also increases parallel to the percentage of intestinal tract that is affected by the disease.

Having never previously heard of UC, I began asking as many questions as popped into my head: "How does someone get UC?" "Did I do something to get it?" "Is it contagious?" "How do you treat it?" "How long before it turns into colon cancer?" "How will you know if it does turn into colon cancer?" "Can this kill me?" The answers to my questions are fairly straightforward: There is no known cause for UC though some physicians believe it to be an autoimmune disease that may be trigged by any number of environmental factors. There was nothing I did that could have caused me to contract or develop it—just luck of the draw, I guess. UC can be managed with medication and routine examinations in conjunction with an annual colonoscopy (Oh, goodie!). The doctor noted that my risk for colon cancer, due to the length of my intestinal tract affected by UC, would infinitely multiply after ten years.

I was first prescribed an oral steroid (an anti-inflammatory) called Prednisone in order to force down the inflammation throughout my intestines. Prednisone is also used to treat other chronic conditions such as asthma, emphysema, and arthritis. My originally prescribed dose was 60 milligrams (mg) per day, which was enough for a horse, or so it seemed. The side effects of Prednisone include increased blood pressure and cholesterol, increased appetite, mood swings, edema (water retention in the body) and headaches among other more serious complications such as premature arteriosclerosis (narrowing of the blood vessels by fat), cataracts, glaucoma, diabetes, osteoporosis and avascular necrosis of bone (a disease that results from loss of blood to the bone causing the bone tissue to die and the bone to collapse).

While taking Prednisone, my blood pressure did soar to an unhealthy level, as did my appetite and the general volatility of my emotional state. I remember coming home from work one night and feeling absolutely famished—starving hungry. In one sitting I devoured an entire pound of pasta and sauce, a peanut butter and jelly sandwich, and a bag of pretzels.

In fairness, however, Prednisone worked wonders for me. Despite its unpredictable and rather unsavory side effects, the symptoms I experienced were mild when compared to what others on a sustained high dosage might suffer. Steroids in general can only serve as a bandage to any underlying health condition and in order to keep my UC in check, I needed to find an alternative maintenance medication that could provide a more permanent solution.

It was then that the doctor prescribed me a drug called mercaptopurine (marketed under the name Purinethol) and also commonly called "6 MP." If you research mercaptopurine on www.drugs.com, you will find the following description:

> *Mercaptopurine is a cancer medication that interferes with the growth of cancer cells and slows their growth and spread in the body. Mercaptopurine may also be used for purposes other than those listed in this medication guide.*[1*]

That is a pretty heavy description for someone who doesn't even have cancer.

After several failed attempts with other drugs, I was not at all confident that 6 MP could work for me. Though as days turned into weeks, months turned into a year, and a year eventually became eight years, it was clear that 6 MP was my miracle drug. It kept the UC in check and managed my pain efficiently while largely eliminating bathroom emergencies. My life would be vastly different, had it not been for 6 MP.

Like all drugs, 6 MP also had its share of side effects. I was required to have blood drawn routinely every three months to ensure that as an immunosuppressant, the 6 MP was not having an effect on the rest of my body. For those of you with a strong aversion to needles or the sight of blood, I would advise you to contract a disease other than Ulcerative Colitis!

1*Mercaptopurine medical facts. Accessed June, 2007.
www.drugs.com/mtm/mercaptopurine.html.

Reflecting on the early days of my colitis is dreadful; I find it hard to believe that I sustained so much pain and discomfort for so long prior to discovering 6 MP. Then the tables turned, and my UC became almost a non-issue while taking steady doses of it. I played competitive sports, I went to the gym, I lifted weights, I skied, I golfed, I biked—nothing was out of bounds. I felt I was fortunate from the perspective that although I had a disease, it was under control, easily manageable, and did not interfere with my normal lifestyle.

During the first two years after being diagnosed with UC, I became a veteran of the disease, learning as much as I could absorb from a medical as well as personal perspective. Knowing all that you can about a disease reduces "surprises" and helps to facilitate more multi-faceted discussions with your physician. In my particular case, memorizing and being actively familiar with the anatomy of the digestive system increased my awareness of what my body was doing, and the possible reasons why.

From a personal perspective, I learned how to gauge my body's reaction to medication, food, drink and physical exertion. In terms of maintaining a normal exercise regimen, the only real issue I had was with working the core area of my body. Intense abdominal sets were not a good idea. I found that I could eat a great variety of food, so long as I moderated my intake of saturated fats, dairy and spicy food. Although most likely every gastroenterologist would advise those suffering with colitis not to drink alcohol, I did, fairly often. I also learned that living with UC requires planning—whether I liked it or not. It is extremely important that you always have your medication nearby when traveling and to be aware of your surroundings, taking mental note of where the nearest bathrooms are and how long it might take to get there. These necessities are inconvenient, but the disease becomes much more manageable when you work with it, as opposed to fighting it.

One thing I would caution against is the use of the internet as a substitute for the advice of a medical professional. The amount of information can be overwhelming and neither always correct, nor regularly updated to reflect the most recent advances in the medical world. It can be useful once you are informed and know what type of information to seek out, but never use it as a tool for diagnosis. I made this mistake and was put through unspeakable emotional stress as I feared that I had HIV due to the symptoms I entered into a website.

As you can imagine, everything I learned about UC and how to live a fulfilling life with the disease was a process of trial and error (more error than not). Keep in mind that each person is different and will react differently to various stimuli. I encourage you to continuously try new things. It's also helpful to record your experiences in a log or journal with the corresponding outcomes for future reference. This also assists the doctor in forming the patterns of your disease and how it might react to food, medication, environment or exertion based on what was successful in the past and what was not.

If there is even the slightest chance that someone may benefit from my experience, then I consider having gone through such a difficult ordeal highly worth it. I heard relatively recently that there are approximately 700,000 people in the United States who suffer from UC. I'll be damned if I let any one of those people do it alone.

Chapter 6:
Second Opinion

I MET A WOMAN, SUE, at work in the fall of 1997. We went out a few times and grew close very quickly. I soon found myself hopelessly head over heels—and just as confused, since I thought the woman I had been seeing for five years prior to meeting Sue was the person I was supposed to settle with. My conflicted feelings and an inability to commit pushed Sue away, truly away—as in across the Atlantic Ocean. In 1999, Sue signed a three-year contract to work in London and Ireland.

I spent the next year completely unhappy with myself. I missed Sue, and knew it was my fault that she chose to leave. Not having her around made everything seem empty and void of meaning in all aspects of my life. With Sue at least two years away from coming home, I wanted to do something with my time that would put me back on track. I had always wanted to earn an MBA, so I figured this was a good time since working toward the MBA was a two-year commitment. My hope was that by the time I had finished, Sue would return and we could be together.

I hung around work to collect my bonus in January of 2001, and quit one month later. I took the GMATs, the standardized test to get into graduate business school, completed several grad school applications, and waited for word if I was accepted. It was at that time that my most recent blood tests indicated "fluctuating liver enzymes that may require further analysis." I was unfamiliar with liver enzymes, why fluctuating enzymes were a concern, and what they could possibly mean for me.

When I met with the doctor to discuss the situation, I asked the most direct and pointed questions I could conceive: "I don't understand what you mean when you say my liver enzymes are fluctuating." The doctor explained that my liver enzymes indicated how well my liver was functioning but that having elevated liver enzymes indicated there may be a problem with the liver. I thought, "Ok, why would I be having a problem with my liver?"

The doctor continued saying, "Your previous blood work showed that your liver enzymes were slightly elevated, then returned to normal levels. Based on your latest round of blood work, your liver enzymes are elevated again, and may require further analysis." The tone was serious and I started to get nervous. I asked, "So what do you think could cause them to fluctuate?" The doctor simply confirmed that additional tests would have to be done to know for sure.

Always curious as to what the underlying cause might be so I could mentally and physically prepare for whatever was in store, I asked, "So what do you think it could be? I'm sure you have some idea?"

The doctor skirted the issue, saying, " I really don't know. We should do a few more rounds of blood work to see if there is a pattern." I called bull shit on the doctor right then as I knew he had an idea of what the cause was, otherwise,

Second Opinion

how would he know to look for a "pattern"? Exactly what kind of pattern was he looking for?

Like a wise ass I asked, "So what if there is a pattern?" Again, in a heaping pile of bull shit, the doctor said, "We'll cross that bridge when we get to it." Great, so I'll get more blood work, see if there is a pattern, and wait for the doctor to decide if he is going to tell me what is really going on. It was then that I started to lose faith and patience with my doctor. He gave me a prescription for blood work every three months and I left his office.

I discovered through my own research that the blood work I had been having drawn every three months, since I started taking 6 MP, was for the purpose of monitoring the other organs in my body, particularly my liver. 6 MP is an oral form of chemotherapy, and as such requires continuous monitoring by examining the enzyme levels in the blood to ensure sure it isn't destroying other organs. If something outside the norm occurs, such as fluctuating enzyme levels, "further analysis" would be required. Well, further analysis was now required.

The next several months were a confining space of darkness as I watched the blood vials fill one after another while waiting on pins and needles to see whether or not I had been accepted into graduate school. The results of the blood tests continued to show fluctuations, which required yet more blood tests. After landing a decent score on the GMAT and nailing my interviews, I was denied entry to every program for which I applied. Regardless of the fact that I applied within the prescribed timeframes, the classes

57

had already been filled to capacity. I should not have been surprised; MBA graduates at that time were still commanding a premium in the marketplace despite the "dot-com" stock market crash of 2000.

The revelation of the damage I had caused for myself began to swarm angrily around me as though I had disturbed a nest of hornets—the painful, throbbing stings of my own frustration, disappointment and depression. Sue was gone; I quit a job in which I was making good money; I now had a severely reduced income; it didn't look like I could go to school; I could no longer afford my apartment or health insurance. Once again I found myself desperate, and once again was forced to put aside the pride I thought I should have as a man, and turn to the one person, the only person I truly trusted in hard times, Daddy, the Constant.

In typical Constant fashion, he pledged, once again, his unwavering love and support. I crumbled inside. I tried so hard to keep the pieces together. Daddy knew how disappointed I was, and seeing me in that state must have been very difficult for him. I wasn't the type of kid who ignored my responsibilities, it was just the opposite. I was so responsible that he probably thought I was wound tighter than Hannibal Lecter in a straight jacket, and I was, psychologically. I hated feeling that I had let myself down, but the ultimate defeat was feeling as though I had let Daddy down.

Daddy talked me into moving in with him and Mommy, encouraged me to apply to school early, and even let me sign-up for the gym within his office so I had access to free exercise equipment. I did everything he recommended, including retaking the GMATs, getting a higher score, and applying to schools early. For income, I began collecting unemployment, which paid for my Cobra Insurance and enabled me to continue having blood drawn. Again, I would wait to hear about grad school and blood work results.

The results of the blood work continued to have ill implications, and the gastro decided I should undergo a more invasive test, called an ERCP (Endoscopic Retrograde Cholangiopancreatography). My family and friends all suggested I seek out a second opinion since it was apparent I was no fan of my doctor. Although I wasn't in love with this gastro, and it didn't seem that he cared too much for me either, I was concerned about switching doctors mid-stream and so was hesitant. Then, seemingly out of nowhere, I received a phone call from Aunt Joann. I hadn't spoken to her in far too long and at that moment in time, her voice sounded more like that of a guardian angel. She asked how I was feeling and about what had been happening. I told her everything I knew and hoped she would tell me in return that everything was fine, but she didn't. Instead, we talked for a long while and she gave me a lot of excellent information. She suggested I contact the Hospital of the University of Pennsylvania (HUP), or UPenn as my family and I had come to call it since that was where John had first gone for treatment. UPenn's reputation preceded it, but I didn't know much about the quality of its medical services and it didn't much matter—if it had Aunt Joann's stamp of approval, I was ready to make an appointment.

I must have sounded like an idiot when I first called the 1-800-789-PENN number. As I fumbled my way through the touch-tone system and finally got in touch with a real person in the department of gastroenterology, I told the woman who answered the phone that I was a new patient and needed to schedule an ERCP, as if this were an everyday event. I fully expected her to say, "Ok, when would you like to come in?" and for that to be the end of it. However, that wasn't the case. She began to ask me why I thought I needed an ERCP, why I needed a gastroenterologist, what outstanding medical issues I had, and if I had ever been seen by someone at UPenn. Incredulous at her probing into my condition as though she cared, I answered her questions as directly as I could and learned the comforting lesson that in high-caliber hospitals of excellent repute such as UPenn, you don't just walk in and out through the revolving door, you become part of the family.

After speaking with the woman for a while, I was very impressed with her knowledge of gastroenterology and its typical procedures, and was able to convince her that I needed to have the ERCP. She finally said, "We have a team of doctors here who specialize in procedures like the ERCP so I'll put you in touch with one of them." She politely placed me on hold and returned a few moments later with a list of four physicians, all on the same team and all had a concentration in ERCP and ECRP-like procedures. After hearing the list of names, I chose the doctor who, in my opinion, sounded like the team leader. His name was Dr. Greg Ginsberg.

I asked my best friend, Tooch, to take me to the ERCP.

I had been friends with Tooch ever since my family moved to Bayville in1986, was the best man at his wedding, and earned the nickname, "JOTS," which stood for Johnny on the Spot when Tooch's Dad passed away in 2000. I would normally have asked my dad to go but I was at odds with my parents at the time. Mommy wasn't pleased with me for being out of work, living at home again, not having much money, and now having increasingly concerning medical problems. Although she had every right to be displeased with me for my recent failures, I did not feel that Mommy had the right by default to dictate to me what I should do about my health, which left Daddy in the middle. Having Tooch take me ensured Daddy could remain neutral.

On the day of the ERCP, Tooch and I arrived at the hospital with plenty of time to register, have my insurance validated and fill out paperwork. I was floored by all the questions I was asked, not only about my personal medical background, but that of my entire immediate family including my brother, sisters, parents and grandparents. The questions were so in-depth that I couldn't even answer some of them. One thing I'll never forget was my written response to the question, "Who is here with you today?" I innocently wrote, "My friend, Paul." He and I got a big kick out of that since we joked that whomever was reading it probably raised an eyebrow, which in reality, I feel absolutely positive did not occur. We carried on to pass the time that I should have written "domestic partner," "prison cell-mate" and other assorted off-color terms for male relationships. If for no other reason, the joking took my mind off of yet another impending medical procedure.

When my name was called, Tooch said, "I'll be right here, Honey, when you get back." I blew him a kiss and said, "Wish me luck!"

I was escorted to a room down a long hall that opened into what seemed like a whole other world. There were two rows of gurneys on either side of the room with hospital curtains hanging from the ceiling separating one gurney from the next. The nurse took me to the first open gurney and drew the curtain. She instructed me to remove everything but my underwear and put on the supplied hospital robe. I was able to leave my socks on but had to place on top some lovely, powder blue "sockettes" on my feet   (I have no idea what they're really called—I just know that the hospital requires you to wear them to protect the sterile environments from the germs on your feet). With regard to the hospital gown, the one thing I can say is that HUP gets it—I don't consider myself a big guy, but I'm definitely not small, either, at about 5'10" and 205 pounds. I fully expected the hospital gown to fit more like a vest than a gown, but to my surprise, it comfortably wrapped all the way around my body and neatly tied shut on the side without my goods hanging out in the front or the back.

I sat on the gurney and pulled the cover sheet up to my waist. There wasn't much to do at this point but wait. The IV nurse came and prepared the setup that would later administer a sedative. No problem, I thought. I had been stuck by so many needles by that time that I considered it a non-event. Tough guy. As the nurse searched for a vein along the back of my hand, an unsuccessful second turned into thirty and I quietly said to her, "I think I'm going to pass out." She immediately removed the needle and flattened my gurney while apologizing profusely for not being able to find the vein on the first try. She was overly hard on herself, and more than sympathetic toward me. Eventually, I felt better, the IV was set, and I could relax until I was called.

As I lay there waiting, I tried to find patterns in the tiled ceiling to distract my myself from anxiously contemplating the ERCP, quite similar to my habit of attempting to find pleasantries in the wallpaper before a rectal exam.

When my name was called about 20 minutes later, I was wheeled into the room where the ERCP would take place. The room was being prepared by a nurse who momentarily stopped what she was doing when I first entered, confirmed that I was the right patient and had me recite my name and birthday two or three times. I was then equipped with a blood pressure cuff, an oxygen gauge, and some type of mouthpiece that hung loosely around my neck. After these preliminaries the nurse paged the doctor to tell him I was ready.

While waiting for the doctor, an anesthesiologist was also in the room who asked me questions as to why I needed the ERCP and other polite chatter. He explained the type of anesthesia I would receive and the effects it would have. I was rather excited, since if it was anything like what you receive prior to a colonoscopy, it would be comforting. I'm probably one of the very few odd people who enjoyed being sedated. It always brought me to a dark, but peaceful place and state of mind that I could never attain while conscious.

When Dr. Ginsberg walked into the room, he was poetry in motion. He exuded confidence without pretension. He was dressed in a pristine blue suit and red tie, with the traditional white, doctor coat over the suit. I was in awe of his fluidity, his focus, and his demeanor. As these thoughts ran through my head, he asked for my chart and walked over to shake my hand. He sat down next to me and said, "Hi, I'm Dr. Ginsberg." Like a teenager meeting a teen idol, I managed a simple, "Hi, I'm Dan Bonner." Dr. Ginsberg then asked why I was having the ERCP done. I told him my story, my history of colitis and the fluctuating liver enzymes.

Dr. Ginsberg then paused and said, "Wait a second. I have never seen you in my office, so how did you get this procedure approved?" I replied, "Well, the gastroenterologist I normally see wanted me to have this done, but I wanted to have it performed here, so I called and scheduled it over the phone."

Dr. Ginsberg put my chart down and sat close to me, saying, "Then we need to talk for a minute." He took the mouth guard from around my neck and positioned me well enough to have a civil conversation with him. He reproved me by saying, "I don't do these procedures unless I have seen you in my office. I need to understand your medical history, view test results, and make a determination if this procedure is even appropriate or not. I'm not sure we should be doing this today."

Feeling as though I had already let him down, and highly concerned that he would cancel the procedure, I said, "I'm sorry about that. When I called and talked to the referral nurse, she didn't tell me I needed to set up an office visit first, so I just scheduled the procedure. My doctor wanted me to have the ERCP done at his local office, but I wanted to come here and get a second opinion."

Dr. Ginsberg didn't blink. He said, "Ok, tell me what's been going on." I explained that I'd had ulcerative colitis for several years, and that I was taking 6 MP to manage it. I told him about the trend with my liver enzymes first fluctuating, then rising steadily over the past nine months.

After Dr. Ginsberg finished his line of questioning, he explained to me in a very sophisticated, very succinct, very prolific way, one in which I will not attempt to replicate, that he felt the need for an ERCP was warranted but that I needed to follow-up with him shortly thereafter in his office. I emitted a huge sigh of relief.

Dr. Ginsberg put my paperwork down, had me sign a release document, and informed me of the potential risks: bleeding, sore throat, and the fact that approximately 3% of procedures may result in Pancreatitis. Whatever, I thought to myself, that stuff happens to other people, people who are sick, not me. After signing, Dr. Ginsberg gave the go-ahead to continue prepping me. One of the nurses repositioned the mouthpiece from around my neck, placed my body in the correct position and dimmed the lights. I was given specific instructions not to try and talk until the procedure was over or I was at risk for damaging my vocal cords. The anesthesiologist administered the sedative and I was out.

I awoke suddenly and violently in the middle of the procedure in an UNBELIEVABLE AMOUNT OF PAIN! As I began to become more aware, I realized that the doctor had no idea I was awake. I tried to talk, violating the only rule I was given prior to being put under but quickly realized I couldn't, no matter how hard I tried. Therefore, I banged my fist on the gurney as hard and quickly as I humanly could desperately trying to get someone's attention. Startled, the nurse yelled at me, "Don't talk! Don't talk!" as she tried to restrain me. I heard someone yell, "Can you help with that??" following by a tingling sensation in my face, and I was unconscious again.

The next thing I remember following that incident was lying on the gurney in recovery with the groggy, hazy feeling to which I was accustomed following a sedated procedure. The only difference was the twinge of pain coming from my stomach. It was nothing I couldn't handle so I dismissed it as perhaps some mild nausea from the sedative. The nurse brought me something to drink and something to eat.

When Dr. Ginsberg arrived to talk with me, I was still very hazy. He may or may not have explained what exactly was wrong with me, which I don't think he did, but I wouldn't have remembered anyway. I do remember him telling me to make an appointment to see him in his office as soon as possible—which I took as a bad omen.

Before leaving, he asked how I felt and I said, "Truthfully, my stomach hurts a bit more than I thought it would after the ERCP." Dr. Ginsberg felt around for signs of tenderness but I really didn't flinch much. He gave me very specific instructions to call if I continued to have pain in my stomach or if it worsened as the day drew on. I agreed and began the process of pulling myself together. I just wanted to get out of there, so Tooch could drop me off and get back to his family.

After I dressed and made my way to the waiting room, Tooch asked how I was feeling and I didn't say much beyond that we should get on the road to avoid the traffic.

As we walked, Tooch asked questions like, "How do you think it went?" "What did the doctor say?" and "What do you have to do now?"

We talked as we walked to the car and I gave him the low-down. "Doctor didn't say much; I need to follow-up with him in his office; He said to call if I was having any problems, etc…" and left it at that. As the anesthesia continued to diminish in my system the pain continued to equally increase in my stomach.

No sooner had Tooch pulled out of the parking deck that the pain in my stomach became absolutely searing. I had no idea what could be wrong since this was my first ERCP, and I had no idea if this type of reaction was normal or not. As Tooch drove on, the pain got worse. I thought it might be that I hadn't eaten much, so we stopped at a convenience store where I bought some pretzels and a Gatorade and got back on the road.

After managing to eat some pretzels and drink a few sips of Gatorade, the pain became worse. There were many moments when I thought the pain couldn't possibly get any worse, only for it to intensify with a vengeance. I sat with my seat tilted back squirming for the duration of ride home. Tooch was distraught and kept asking how he could help but there was nothing he could do.

When we walked in the door of my house, I tried to put on a strong face. I didn't want anyone to think I was a wimp, especially Daddy. By 8:00 p.m., I couldn't take it anymore. When I told Daddy that I "wasn't feeling well" he was obviously concerned but I again tried to put on a strong face saying, "I'll let you know if it gets any worse. If it does, we may need to go to the hospital." In true Constant fashion, he said, "Whatever you need." without a hint of sarcasm, only genuine concern.

By 9:30 p.m., I was at my wits end and broken down from the beating my body was taking. I told Daddy, "I can't take it anymore. We have to go to the hospital." He rose up from his chair, grabbed his keys and said, "Let's go. I just have to tell your mother." I strategically waited for my mom to go to bed so she wouldn't be overly concerned. I had always tried to minimize the description of any medical problems for my mom; there were times when I had seen the fear in her eyes when I wasn't well, and I didn't want to alarm her.

I tried to convince Megan that it wasn't worth her time to go, but Megan is the type of person who will walk through hell or high water with whomever is in trouble. She was going and that was the end of it.

When we arrived at the hospital, I went to the front desk to register. By that time I was in so much pain that it was difficult to breathe and therefore difficult to talk. Every time I drew a breath it felt like a hunting knife was stabbed into my stomach and slowly removed when I exhaled.

I tried to sit down after I registered but the pain was too intense. I tried every position I could think of in an effort to find reprieve, but nothing worked. Eventually I discovered that if I knelt on the ground while leaning against the seat with my arms hanging by my side, I could tolerate the pain—so that's where I stayed. It was now 10:00 p.m. It had been over seven hours since leaving UPenn with Tooch.

I soon became vocal with my pain and began grunting through my teeth every time I exhaled. I tried to control the agony I was in as much as I could but each and every breath was so painful that I wished I could stop breathing altogether. I began to get a lot of attention from the other people in the waiting area. I felt their eyes staring at me and I could hear their whispers. One woman said to her husband, "Come on, let's go. I don't feel anywhere near as bad as he does and he should get checked out as soon as possible."

When the nurse finally called my name for vitals, I told her that I'd had an ERCP earlier in the day and the doctor said there was a possibility I could get Pancreatitis from it—I thought this might be exactly that. To my surprise, I had to explain what an ERCP was and why it was performed. Previously, I had assumed that everyone knew what this procedure was but it was much less commonly practiced than I thought. The nurse brought me to the back and changed my priority level for a doctor to come and see me as soon as possible.

When I finally saw the doctor, I took charge like I never had before. I blurted out quickly, "Hi, Doctor. My name is Dan Bonner and I came in because I had an ERCP earlier in the day and haven't felt good since. The doctor who performed the ERCP said that Pancreatitis was one of the possible risks of an ERCP so I need a blood test to see if that's the case. In the mean time, I need a pain killer." I was stunned for a second at what had just poured out of my mouth. I would never have spoken that way to a doctor normally, but I was in no condition to give the nice, friendly version of my story. What worked in my favor was that I sounded like I knew what I was talking about and wasn't disrespectful. It was obvious that I was in a tremendous amount of pain. After a quick explanation of my history with UC and fluctuating liver enzymes, the doctor was satisfied and went on his way. Within five minutes, a nurse came to start an IV and as soon as it was ready, the doctor was there with a shot of morphine. The morphine hit my blood stream and in seconds the pain was gone. I fell in love with pain killers at that very moment.

After about 20 minutes, I started to feel a twinge in my stomach again. I asked the nurse if I could have more morphine but I was denied. The span of time between the initial injection and my request for a second was too close. This time the pain increased exponentially over the next ten minutes and spiraled completely out of control. I was squirming all over the gurney in complete and total agony. The doctor came and asked how I would rate my pain and after disclosing to him that on a scale of 10 it was a 25, he surmised morphine did not do much for me and so brought an injection of Demerol. Demerol is now, and will always be, my pain killer of choice.

It was unbelievable how (almost disturbingly) well the Demerol worked; and not just from the standpoint of how quickly the pain disappeared, but how incredible you feel once the drug hits your bloodstream. I felt as if I could jump off that gurney and run a marathon. It was also at this very moment that I realized how and why people become addicted to pain killers. I was deeply relaxed and felt reeeeeeally gooooooooooooooooood (read that line very slowly—that was exactly how I felt).

When my testing results were available, the doctor informed me that I did indeed have Pancreatitis. My pancreatic enzyme level was in the 11,000 range—a normal range is from 0 to 60. Now that I had been officially diagnosed with Pancreatitis, I was admitted to the hospital.

The night I was hospitalized with Pancreatitis was only the second time I ever had been admitted. The first time was when I was a junior in high school. I walked out of my last period class, went to talk to my girlfriend, and suddenly developed heart palpitations, dizziness, and weakness in my arms and legs. I was taken to the emergency room, where I was admitted, given a barrage of tests, spent a few days, and was released. I was diagnosed as having a minor heart murmur, although looking back, I personally believe it was an anxiety attack.

This hospital stay was a far different story. There were doctors coming in to check on me constantly, I was in excruciating pain and I couldn't eat solid food. Pancreatitis is typically treated with IV fluids, pain killers, and no solids. I had gone 24 hours without eating anything for colonoscopies, but never multiple days. It was a very new, and very odd, sensation to fast for days at a time. One of the doctors who came to meet with me was a gastro, Dr. Rangas Lokchander. He was of Indian descent, somewhat short in stature, and almost impossible to understand. Dr. Lokchander would come in, check my enzyme levels, ask me questions, and make sure I had everything I needed. His bedside manner was comforting during a time when I was the least comfortable I had ever been.

Over the next couple of days, my pancreatic enzymes dropped and I was able to go home. Dr. Lokchander stopped in to see me before I left and asked who my primary care physician was. I told him I wasn't happy with my primary gastroenterologist and that Dr. Ginsberg did my ERCP at HUP. Dr. Lokchander then took out a card and said, "Here, take my card. Feel free to call me anytime if you have questions or would like another opinion." He said it in such a way that wasn't arrogant, forward, or in a tone that could be construed as fishing for business; he sounded sincere and like he genuinely cared about my condition. I appreciated that a great deal, especially within the context of being shuffled between different physicians and never truly being happy with any one of them.

I took Dr. Lokchander up on his offer and called his office. His assistant, Dori, was an absolute sweetheart from day one. She politely provided me with directions to the office and tolerated my fumbling over the pronunciation of her name.

When I arrived, the waiting area was crowded with patients, all of whom looked like they had just escaped from the local nursing home and robbed the blue-hair wig shop on the way over. I was the youngest patient in the room easily by three or four decades. As I looked at them wondering what could possibly be wrong with all of them, I felt them looking back at me, probably wondering the same thing, minus a stop at the wig shop.

When Dr. Lokchander came into the exam room, he shook my hand and asked how I was doing. I grew used to his accent while I was in the hospital, but was struggling again to understand what he was saying. Within a few minutes I was able to understand him more clearly and seemed to forget that he had an accent at all.

He began by asking me a lot of questions in order to gain perspective on my medical history. He sat and took notes as I talked and asked me to elaborate when he needed further information. When I said something that made no sense to him, he asked for clarification. The questions flowed from him naturally—he never needed to search for the right choice of words and never seemed to feel uncomfortable. He also, and I will forever be appreciative of this, never made me feel rushed, as though my examination were a get-in-get-out affair.

I continued to see Dr. Lokchander for some time while "officially" retaining my original gastroenterologist; I wasn't sure about "politeness protocol" in terms of permanently severing ties with a physician. I struggled with the thought of returning to him out of loyalty despite the fact that I didn't care for him as a doctor. The more I got to know Dr. Lokchander, however, the easier it became to distance myself from the original gastro. Finally, I made a decision: I called the original gastro and requested to have my records sent to Dr. Lokchander. If I was doomed to go through hell at some point in the future, I wanted a doctor by my side that would be there for me every step of the way and I felt that I had found that in Dr. Lokchander.

I was confident that I had made the right decision. I became friends with Dori and finally started calling her by her first name; I met and became friends with Donna, Dr. Lokchander's nurse. My visits became more conversational than stodgy doctor/patient interactions. When I made appointments to see Dr. Lokchander, I would end up talking with Dori or Donna on the phone for a spell and would continue the conversation when I got to the office. We would exchange stories of where we had gone on vacation, what we had been doing, who we were dating or not dating, and at some point Dori and Donna would always ask how I was feeling. My usual reply was "Fine." and we would continue talking.

I continue to see Dr. Lokchander to this day. Upon a recent visit for my annual colonoscopy and endoscopy, he discovered a subcutaneous lesion in my esophagus and thought it would be in my best interest to contact UPenn and ask for their input. Whenever I call Dr. Lokchander's office, I have the great fortune of getting to speak to either Donna or Dori. It's a pleasure to connect to a real human being on the phone rather than a response service or a self-absorbed college student.

I believe Dr. Lokchander answered his calling in life when he chose to become a doctor and I'm thankful that we found each other. Had I stayed at UPenn after the ERCP, I would never have met Dr. Lokchander and may have continued to see a doctor with whom I had no relationship. I will always be grateful to Dr. Lokchander, Dori, Donna, and the powers that brought us together.

Chapter 7:
It's Got a Name

"D-DAY" ARRIVED IN JANUARY of 2002—the day I was scheduled to see Dr. Ginsberg and hear the results of the ERCP test and the diagnosis for my liver. During the drive to UPenn, I was cocky. By that point I thought that nothing could be worse than already having UC and I would be able to shake it off. I was sick and tired of having blood tests drawn religiously and bouncing liver enzymes; all I wanted to know was the real diagnosis and how to fix it while trying to move on with my life.

Dr. Ginsberg and I exchanged basic pleasantries before diving into why I was actually there. I told him about getting pancreatitis after the ERCP and having to spend some time in the hospital. He was overly hard on himself, saying that he had gone against his better judgment by letting me go home that day rather than admitting me. I never blamed him—I feel certain that fate intervened that day and brought me together with Dr. Lokchander.

Dr. Ginsberg thanked me for my understanding with the whole situation. Meanwhile, I thought, "Please. You are the venerable Dr. Ginsberg who has a reputation for being the Jesus Christ of ERCPs, so I don't really care what happened; you could give me another ERCP right now if you want using a rusty spoon and a paper clip and I wouldn't care." I could see that Dr. Ginsberg was combing over the situation, rotating it in his memory and examining it from various angles, but it really was fine. He shouldn't have been so hard on himself.

Prior to commencing his explanation of what had been discovered during the procedure, Dr. Ginsberg explained that I would probably have a lot of questions to ask, but to try and hold them until the end of the discussion. He first walked through a quick debriefing of the procedure: a tube was placed down my throat and guided to my liver; once he had navigated to my liver, dye was injected and x-ray type images were taken in order to view the passageways of the liver. By the time he had completed his thorough explanation, my anxiety was nearly overwhelming.

After he finished describing the procedure, he said something along the lines of, "I was able to determine that you have a liver disease called Primary Sclerosing Cholangitis or PSC for short; have you ever heard of it?" I thought, "Actually I had sclerosed my cholanwhateveryoujustsaid last week—NO I NEVER HEARD OF IT!" But responded, "No, I can't say that I have." He explained that PSC is a debilitating disease that causes the bile ducts in the liver to close, eventually causing liver failure. I can only imagine the look of vacancy on my face since I didn't understand a word he said. It didn't sound like this was something I would be able to knock out quickly and I began to rethink whether cocky was the right approach after all.

I sat there listening very intently to Dr. Ginsberg, who was the consummate professional, delivering my bad news in a stoic way with integrity and lucidity. As he spoke, I tried to remember everything he was saying. That was a bad decision, since as soon as I would attempt to conceptualize some term or other that he said, the space of time it took me to do that placed me further and further behind Dr. Ginsberg's explanation. I retained less and less information until it seemed as if he were speaking another language, at which point I shut down. I heard words I had never before heard, conditions with which I was not even in the same neighborhood of familiarity, and parts of the body I never knew existed. In retrospect it would have been a smart idea to bring a listening companion, someone to sit there and help me absorb all the information being thrown at me.

Recognizing the seriousness of the situation, I tried to come up with an intelligent question. I picked up on the liver failure part and presumed the disease would never reach that degree if treated properly, but had to ask the one question that always came to mind when things got this heavy: "Is it fatal?" His reply was laconic yet stunning: "It could be." I felt the blood rush from my brain toward my feet, as if it were trying to find a dark place in which to safely hide away. I presumed that it was my body's physiological response to denial. However, as I sat there frozen, not saying anything, Dr. Ginsberg, the accomplished professional that he was, continued with his explanation. It was obvious that this wasn't the first time he had delivered bad news, and I was grateful for his finesse and professionalism, which seemed to carry me somewhat through the moment.

Dr. Ginsberg delved into precisely how the disease progresses slowly over time, causing a lot of damage to the liver, which in turn begins to shut down—eventually shutting down completely. If that happened, the PSC would definitely have the potential to kill me. Luckily for me, he said, the disease was caught very early, so close monitoring should allow it to be treated correctly.

I thought, "That sounds promising. At least I'll never make it to the 'fatal' stage. It was caught early and therefore it should be treatable. I can breathe a sigh of relief." My next question was, "Ok, how is it treated?" Dr. Ginsberg replied very intently and seriously that there is no known cure for PSC, except for liver transplantation. I don't actually recall those words coming out of his mouth since I was in shock. It seemed surreal at the time and even more surreal now. I thought for a fleeting moment that I had dodged the "fatal" bullet but it snapped right back like a boomerang.

I asked Dr. Ginsberg how sure he was of the diagnosis and if a transplant was really the only treatment. He was very sure. The disease progresses differently in each individual so I was given a range of 3-10 years, maybe even longer, before I would require the transplant. He made it clear to me, though, that the transplant was imminent.

I had a lot of research ahead of me on a topic entirely separate from the hours upon hours I had spent just researching UC. I also remember Dr. Ginsberg telling me that I would need to talk with the liver transplant team at UPenn at some point, but there was no way to be sure exactly when that would need to be. The last thing I remember before leaving the examination room was one last awe-inspiring act by Dr. Ginsberg: in order to properly communicate what we talked about, he picked up the phone hanging on the wall, dialed a number, and began to give an oral synopsis of my examination. He spoke in beautifully constructed sentences, never hesitating with a thought, never stumbling over his words, and never struggling to find the right words. His intelligence was staggering to me.

After he had completed the synopsis, he provided me with some basic instructions that involved scheduling a follow-up appointment, the phone number to his nurse, and encouraged me to call with any questions or concerns. I thanked him, shook his hand, and left. I stopped at the desk, gave the woman my paperwork, and scheduled an appointment for some point in the future.

As I walked out of the office, I felt listless and utterly drained. I was overcome with a barrage of racing thoughts that refused to cease even for one single moment, housed within an achingly tired physical vehicle. I wanted to stop but I couldn't; I wanted to focus on one thought at a time; I couldn't. Eventually, I wanted to stop thinking entirely, and couldn't. I was trapped within a cycle of continuously torturous and anticlimactic, chaotic thoughts. I wondered, "How did I get this?" "Since when did I become so unhealthy?" "What about grad school?" "How am I going to tell Mommy and Daddy?" "What about Sue?" "How am I going to tell the rest of the family?" I was drowning— drowning within the cruel quick sand of my own thoughts. During the drive home, my mind was nothing but a vast empty space.

That night was a blur. I'm sure when I got home, I must have told my parents what was going on. However, I know nothing of the words I chose or what their reaction was. Those details seem to be caught in the space between dreams and reality. There was simply too much to process that night, hence my lack of memory. I had entirely shut down.

The only thing I remember from that night is sitting on the couch watching TV with my dad after my mom went to bed. We sat there, in silence, watching the *Lone Ranger* and the *Gene Autry Show*, two of Daddy's favorites. In typical fashion, he could sense that I wasn't right and asked, "You ok?" I said, "Yeah, I'm fine. We'll just have to see what happens." "You know I'm always here for you if you need anything." Daddy said. That brought a sense of comfort to my psyche and quieted my mind, if only temporarily. I never expected him to say or do the things that he always did; and I certainly did not deserve his tremendous and unlimited love and support. He was consistent. He was the Constant, and he was more than willing to take the burdens from my bruised shoulders and bear them upon his own.

When I went to bed that night, I really wasn't tired. I remember lying in bed staring up at the ceiling, looking for patterns and pleasantries as I usually did when I was in the throes of a stressful situation. I thought about how "D-Day" didn't really turn out as I had originally planned but at least my condition now had a name.

In rapid succession, question after question began pouring through the floodgates of my mind: Is there anything I can do to prevent this from happening? If not, how long would it be before I got transplanted: three years, five years, ten years, or maybe more if I can hold out long enough? Would I ever even need a transplant if there are advances in medicine? What happens if I go to school and need a transplant in the middle of a semester? How do I even go about finding another liver? What happens if I don't get a liver in time—will the hospital just let me die? What if I do die? There are still so many things I want to do in life. I want to get married, have kids and grandkids. This just doesn't seem right. If I do die, will people even come to my funeral? Will I get to heaven? I don't know if I've been good enough to get there. Is there even an afterlife? I believe in God but we haven't been on the best of terms recently. How am I going to tell the rest of the family? How do I even begin to tell OB, Bridget and Megan? If I get the transplant, what will happen after that? Will I be well enough to get married and have kids? It wasn't easy for John when he was transplanted, so how hard will it be on me? At that moment I felt the slam of an anchor in my chest: "Oh, my God! John!"

The realization that John died at the age of 29 after having gone through two liver transplants was enough to physically immobilize me. The wave of emotions was too great for me to handle and my body began to physically shut down. As new thoughts filled my brain, my body decided it had had enough for the day, my eyes closed, and I fell to sleep. Sleep was the last thing I wanted at that moment, but my body gave me no choice.

I woke the next morning feeling really low. I had to figure out how to tell OB, Bridget, Megan, and the rest of the family about the PSC diagnosis and what would most likely be in store for me. I thought about John more than I had in years and wondered how he was able to have his initial transplant and why he needed a second. I wondered how Uncle Pete, Aunt Joann, Mary Jo, Amy and Peter dealt with his passing. I thought about how much of a resource John could have been for me if he were still alive. I thought about how unlikely it seemed for two people who lived next-door to each other to both require liver transplants, and if there were some external factors that may have contributed to that. The odds just seemed too great.

I had to find out exactly what John's story was and how it compared to my own. I was reluctant to call Uncle Pete and Aunt Joann to ask them, since I didn't want to cause them unnecessary suffering by prodding over events from the past. I didn't want to tear open old wounds, especially if they had only begun to heal. I chose to talk to my parents to see what they remembered.

My parents said that John was diagnosed with UC as a young teen, around 15 or 16 years old. He had the same type of colitis that I did, involving infection of the entire colon. John's colitis, however, was more aggressive, and did not respond as well to medication. After John had colitis for several years, he also developed a liver condition, Primary Sclerosing Cholangitis, which was why he needed his first liver transplant.

I was in such a state of denial, and such a state of déjá vu, that I couldn't speak. How was it even conceivable that John and I could have the same diseases? How was it that I didn't put two and two together earlier? Why didn't my parents bring this to my attention sooner? Regardless, the similarities between John and I are astounding. If the two of us having the same exact diseases, in the same order, was nothing but a roll of the dice with no external association or factors, it has to be one of the most unbelievable coincidences in modern medicine.

Knowing the similarities between John and I made me feel that I was staring down a death sentence. Concerned that news would break shortly throughout the family, I wanted to get in touch with OB, Bridget, and Megan before they heard about it from anyone else. I didn't know if I was dying or not, but I certainly didn't want them to think that I was.

I told OB and a group of my friends, Tom, Chris, and Gregg, all at the same time. That was a difficult conversation. There were many questions, and even among us guys, many tears. I spoke to my two sisters, Bridget and Megan, separately.

Having kept in close contact with Sue while she was away, I wanted to see her in person to tell her what was going on. I scheduled a trip to London that February. While I was there, we had many heavy conversations about the disease, and about us. In between very emotional discussions, Sue and I still had a good time. We went to see "Monsters, Inc." in the theater and splurged on the popcorn and candy combo, which included a huge bag of peanut M&M's. We ate like a couple of FS's (our private abbreviation for "fat shits") and had a great evening. Sue also treated me to a traditional English breakfast with baked beans and blood pudding, which I thought was interesting as a breakfast, although I'll never order that again. The remaining details of that trip are deeply personal. It became apparent that even the ocean was not able to truly separate Sue and me, and we always managed to find one another, despite the very worst of circumstances. Still to this day, the wounds are easily reopened thinking about how difficult it was to say goodbye to Sue and how difficult it was for us to be torn apart as I stepped onto the plane. Once the pain of departure settled, the connection between us would reestablish itself, and we knew it was only a matter of time before we would come together once more.

Once I was home, I scheduled a trip to Mississippi to see Uncle Pete, Aunt Joann, Mary Jo, Amy and Peter. I wanted to see them and take the first step in sharing the journey that both John I had now undertaken. It was good to reconnect as old friends and family who hadn't seen each other in a while. It had been far too long.

Before leaving for Mississippi, I received an acceptance letter from Pennsylvania State University to begin my MBA program in August. That letter took a tremendous amount of weight from my mind. If I didn't know what my future had in store from a physical standpoint, I could at least head to graduate school if I stayed healthy.

When I stepped off the plane in Mississippi, Uncle Pete and Aunt Joann were there to pick me up. They looked exactly as I had remembered them. Uncle Pete always had the handshake of a lumberjack and hugged like a bear. It was a different story with Aunt Joann: she was very petite and I was afraid I would break her if I hugged her too hard. I hugged her hard anyway.

We stopped for lunch on the way home and arrived at their house in the early afternoon. John's old truck was in the driveway, which I later discovered Aunt Joann would drive every now and then. They had kept it in working order. Memories of playing home run derby, four-wheeling and being dropped at home after work by John appeared vividly in my mind. Not having John here now was especially bittersweet, knowing that I may well share his fate.

Uncle Pete and Aunt Joann told me that Mary Jo lived nearby with her family, Peter lived close by with his family, and Amy would be driving down from Jackson with her two kids to stay at the house as well. I was nervously excited to see everyone, realizing that this scenario was far different from playing altogether on Tudor Drive in Toms River. Mary Jo was married with two kids, Amy was married with two kids, and Peter was married with four kids. I looked forward greatly to meeting the next generation of Sciarabbas.

People began pouring into the house shortly after we arrived. Mary Jo looked absolutely amazing. She had light brown hair with blonde highlights and a smile that lit up the room. Her husband, Derek, was a huge guy, over 6 feet tall and 300 pounds. I joked with him that I could take him in a wrestling match. That was enough to fire him up and we were horsing around moments later. I got the distinct impression he was taking it easy on me, as he could have quite easily picked me up and thrown me across the room had he wanted to. He was a great guy.

Amy arrived shortly thereafter with her two kids. Just like Mary Jo, Amy was a knockout and passed her good looks onto her daughter. Amy's husband, Drew, had come down for a while but had to go home and run the family business. Another great guy.

I was able to meet Peter's wife, Rebecca, before I even got to see Peter. Uncle Pete owned a lawn mower sales and repair service shop where Peter's wife Rebecca worked. She emanated warmth and compassion and was a pure delight. I saw Peter and met his kids later that evening. Peter had long blonde hair, long enough to put into a pony tail and was more strapping than I remember. He had been working for a landscaping business and was in great shape.

My time with the Sciarabbas was like a family reunion. It was wonderful. Eventually, we settled in to talk about John so I could compare notes. Mary Jo, Amy, and Peter were all there, and we discussed the similarities and any differences between the development of John's illness and my own. Knowing what little bit I did about John was enough to keep my nerves on high alert.

The similarities between us were uncanny. We both had colitis of the entire colon and were both diagnosed with PSC. Neither of us had a history of either disease in our respective families. This seemed particularly troubling since both colitis and PSC are autoimmune diseases that in many cases are traced through lineage.

We also discussed the medical histories of our immediate families, trying to determine if anyone had experienced similar symptoms or conditions. Needless to say, no one had.

The closest we came to a possible connection was my sister Bridget, who has had stomach and/or digestive issues for some time although no official diagnosis was ever made.

It is no secret that Toms River, New Jersey became an infamous hot bed for child cancer cases, spurning multiple law suits, and even a movie starring John Travolta, called "A Civil Action." I didn't know many of the details surrounding the problem, but one of the chemical processing plants close to Toms River, Ciba-Geigy, was accused of mishandling and even "dumping" harmful chemicals on vast amounts of unused farmland within the town of Toms River itself. The theory was that the chemicals had made their way into the water supply, striking many children with various forms of cancer. The lawsuit was eventually settled with the plaintiffs of that case receiving a large sum of money. This information wasn't available until years after both of our families had moved out of Toms River, but it gave Mary Jo an excellent starting point with which to begin an investigation.

Mary Jo was able to uncover an unbelievable amount of information about the Ciba-Geigy case—a mountain of paperwork that included maps, statistics, test results of the surrounding land and water supply, government documents identifying the issues, websites, emails, medical references, and on it went. Mary Jo showed me some compelling maps that identified where our houses were located on Tudor Drive and how close we were to some of the dumping sites. Our houses were situated in the center of a dumping site where the pollution began in the late 1960's and continued through the early 70's. John was born in 1964 and I was born in 1973. It was hidden from us that we lived on top of a chemical biohazard site—close to neighborhoods where children lived and played and families grew, as pregnant women brought their infants trustingly into an unknowingly infected, toxic area. How could we ever have known? It was kept secret from the residents.

Prior to leaving Mississippi, Peter took me to John's grave. John is buried on a small plot of land close to Uncle Pete and Aunt Joann's house. I stood there for a few moments in silence, then said a prayer and asked John to look out for me and the storm clouds on my horizon. It was difficult to look upon the grave of my childhood friend, someone whose death perhaps could have been prevented, and it is difficult to this day not to ask why. It was also difficult for me to stand before him knowing that I could share his fate.

My last night in Mississippi, I wanted to take everyone out to dinner. It was my way of having everyone in the same place where we could share some smiles and good times without thinking about the loss of John or what might be in store for me. I had a great time looking around the table at the friends I had known all my life. As I looked at their families and their kids, it felt good to know that the next generation of Sciarabbas was secure. What began on Tudor Drive as neighbors grew into friends and then family. I knew that no distance would be able to separate us, and every memory I have from that trip is dear to me. I also discovered a newly found connection to John, and asked him for guidance.

Heading home after consecutive trips to see Sue and the Sciarabbas was a double- edged sword – while it was great to see everyone, the road that lay before me became clearer. I knew it was going to be treacherous, petrifying, and physically debilitating. As such, I had to resolve my issues with God as I was surely going to need Him by my side every step of the way. On the plane ride home, I lacked the courage to talk with God directly. I had separated myself from Him for so long that I didn't know what to say.

After going back and forth over how to reinitiate this for some time, with a heavy heart and a huge lump in my throat, I closed my eyes and with all the sincerity I possessed, asked God to forgive me for turning my back on Him. That was the toughest prayer I had ever prayed. Tears welled in my eyes as I felt the spirit of God fill every square inch of my insides. I could feel the comfort of God say directly to me, "It's ok. I've been here all along." I glowed with the warmth of the sun emanating from my body and soul. It felt as if I was already home well before my plane landed.

Chapter 8:
From Penn to Penn

I MOVED TO THE Penn State campus in August, 2002. Mom, Dad, Bridget, her husband, Jarlath, and my nephew, Ryan made the trip along with me to help move things into the apartment. As I pulled in front of the building, I parked the truck behind a guy who was also already well into the process of moving in. I introduced myself, found that his name was Jay, and that he was also here to earn the MBA. We were to live on the same floor and would be seeing a lot of each other.

Moving day was extremely long and tiring. By 6:00 p.m. I was exhausted and forced to lie on the couch while my mom and Bridget tidied up the new apartment. My family stayed with me that night and left the next morning following breakfast. Though I felt relatively well, there was a nagging feeling that something was wrong, something underlying that I couldn't readily identify. I lay back down on the couch and tried to just take it easy, thinking that perhaps I was simply still tired from the stress of the move.

Jay came over and asked if I wanted to take a walk around the campus. I did, since I was eager to see the buildings where class would be held and get a feel for the campus itself before the semester officially began. It was a lovely day—one of those rare early autumnal jewel-of-a-days when the temperature was perfectly balanced between the warm remnants of the passing summer and the slightest chill from the impending winter. Over the next several days, we walked around, met others in the program, and got a general idea of how things would unfold.

All incoming students were scheduled for a week-long first-year orientation. The idea was to help the people within the program meet and become familiar with one-another and facilitate the formation of team projects.

The night before orientation was to commence, I was officially not feeling well and experienced a decrease in appetite. Instead of eating a full dinner, I made myself a peanut butter and jelly sandwich (I probably hold the world record for the most P.B.J. sandwiches ever consumed—I averaged more than two a day beginning when I was five years old), some pretzels, and a Gatorade.

As I stood ironing a shirt, I was slammed suddenly with an intense, sharp pain in my torso that caused my legs to collapse and dropped me to my knees. I said out loud, "What the fuck?" I had no idea what had just happened—I just wanted it to stop. It was an incredible amount of pain that left me breathless, not wanting to even attempt walking to the couch. I crawled, instead, and tried to lie down hoping the pain would subside but it refused. It worsened quickly and I knew I had better get to the hospital. I very slowly made my way down to Jay's apartment to let him know where I was going. He offered to drive, but I didn't want him to go, not having any idea how many hours I might spend there. I also hadn't told him any details surrounding my illness and wanted to keep things private as long as possible.

When I arrived at the entrance to the emergency room, I made my way to the registration desk to give my personal and insurance information, have my blood pressure (BP) and temperature measured, and provide the nurse a history of my ailments. Relaying a history from the early days of colitis until the present took some time, but gave her a fairly thorough understanding and idea as to what might be wrong. The one good thing about having so many painful physical issues was that 99% of the time, when I went to the emergency room, I would go from the registration desk directly to be seen by a physician. The only people who could trump me in the emergency room were gunshot victims, stabbing victims, or victims of car accidents. Other than that, the people who had a bad headache or whooping cough would have to wait.

The nurse rose from her chair to take me to the back, but I simply couldn't walk anymore. As I struggled with each painful breath, the expenditure of energy left me unable to stand, much less walk. Soon after being wheeled to the examination room, a doctor came in while simultaneously looking at my information. He acknowledged that I was in a tremendous amount of pain, asked me to rate it on a scale of one-to-ten, of which it was at least a 12, and to pinpoint where the pain was coming from. After giving him all of this information, he asked without hesitation if there was a particular pain killer that I preferred. I explained to him how morphine didn't do much for me and that I preferred Demerol. He got right on it.

As he walked away I became incredibly nauseous and knew I was going to vomit any second; I needed a "throw-up proof" container, and fast. I looked frantically around the room and found nothing, so into the hazardous waste bin it went. I had no choice. The doctor returned shortly and gave me the injection of Demerol. As it flowed through my system, the pain immediately subsided from a level 12 to a zero in a few short moments. I caught my breath and was able to reply clearly to the doctor when he asked how I felt. I was able to relax for the first time in almost five hours. The initial strike of pain occurred around 6:00 p.m. and it was now nearly 11:00 p.m.

The emergency room doctor informed me that he was trying to get in touch with someone at UPenn for a second opinion. I groggily agreed then immediately fell asleep. Narcotic analgesics always lulled me into a peaceful slumber, for which I was grateful.

Over the next few hours I was half-lucid, trying to figure out in between bouts of sleeping whether or not I would make it to orientation. At some point, the doctor came to tell me that I was being moved to UPenn. I got a little excited, thinking I might get to be sent via helicopter, but not quite. I was instead strapped to a gurney and driven the four-hour distance from Penn State to HUP. Not cool.

I called Jay to let him know that I would never make it to orientation and asked him to tell the administrators on my behalf. I also called my parents, though I haven't much recollection of what was said. I remember only highlights of telling them I was in a lot of pain, went to the ER, and was being sent to UPenn. My parents began firing questions at me, none of which I recall. I do remember telling them that the drive to UPenn was long, so they could go back to sleep and I'd call them later, after which time I hung up the phone while they continued talking. It must have been somewhere between 2:00 or 3:00 a.m. by the time I talked to my parents; I awoke only briefly when I was placed in the back of the ambulance, and briefly when they pulled finally into UPenn.

When we arrived at UPenn, it must have been close to 6:30 or 7:00 a.m. Although doctors from UPenn were expecting me, specifically doctors from the gastroenterology department, I was still placed in a room within the emergency department. Within ten minutes of settling in, my parents walked by with Bridget and Ryan and began asking questions—all highly intelligent, relevant questions— in rapid succession. I quickly got the impression that they thought my liver was failing and I was soon to be on the transplant list.

I hadn't given any thought to what was happening since I had been happily dozing on pain killers for the last several hours. As my family asked questions, I had no idea what was being said in the flurry around me. I just knew I wanted to be strong in their presence, in case it was my liver. I had no answers to any of their questions.

My parents handled the chaotic sequence of events with relative good humor, even sharing a laugh over my hanging up on them while still in the ER at Penn State. They had just taken a guess at when they thought I might arrive at UPenn and started driving.

I encouraged everyone to just relax, go get something to eat and wander back in a while since I was sure it would be some time before a doctor came to examine me. Just as I had completed my sentence, two physicians walked through the door. "Guess I was wrong." I said to my parents.

The first doctor to introduce himself was Dr. Kochman. He explained that Dr. Ginsberg was on vacation, but he was on Dr. Ginsberg's team and was covering his patients. The second doctor, whose name I can't recall, was an extremely attractive blonde woman who was also a member of the gastroenterology department.

Dr. Kochman immediately began asking me questions along the lines of where was the pain? How long had I had the pain? On a scale of $1-10$, how would I rate the pain? Did I eat or drink anything out of the ordinary? Had I ever felt this pain before? I was fully awake by this time and able to answer his questions methodically, since this line of inquiry and I were pretty intimate by this point. Next in line was a round of blood work to ascertain a baseline reading of my liver enzyme numbers.

My parents were now faced with meeting the gastroenterologist for the first time since I had been diagnosed with PSC. There was a brief lull in the conversation as the doctor scribbled some notes and my parents took the opportunity to pounce and fill their minds with all the information I had been denying them. I became nervous when this happened since I made an obsessively concerted effort to stay on top of my condition by reading the latest news articles and scouring the web for all the latest medical innovations. My parents, on the other hand, were approaching the doctor from a concerned parent standpoint that, in the past, occasionally resulted in several questions I could answer myself or worse, a question that would absolutely make me cringe. I don't blame my parents since I'm sure that if it were my child, I would be ten times more irritating. However, on this particular day, all of the questions my parents asked were relevant. I felt ashamed of myself for underestimating them.

When the results from the blood work were returned, everyone was tense. We were all prepared to hear the worst: my liver was failing. Dr. Kochman informed me that with regard to my liver, the numbers were in line with my previous results—whatever was causing the pain wasn't my liver. The only question that remained, then, was what WAS causing the pain if it wasn't the liver; both my parents were quick to ask that key question before I had the chance to vocalize it for myself. At the time, their leap into interrogating the doctor in my stead irritated me a bit, since I was 29 years old, not 12. I was indignant and felt more than capable of handling interactions with my various physicians.

Dr. Kochman explained that there were indicators in the blood work that pointed to my gall bladder as the potential culprit, though additional testing would be required (of course). The tests were scheduled for later that day and I was supremely relieved from the strain of believing that my liver had begun to fail. My greatest fear, had that been the reality, was that graduate school would be reduced to nothing more than a pipe dream.

It was the afternoon, and since tests were tests, I asked my parents to please not worry and go get some lunch. I also hadn't eaten in over 24 hours, and wanted something, anything—a Snickers—I didn't care what it was but having to get tests precluded me from eating.

I was placed on a table where another large, metal table pressed down on me to monitor my gall bladder. A dye was injected, whose purpose it was to illuminate my gall bladder on a screen across the room. If my gall bladder appeared on the screen, then it was in operating order and the cause of my pain was rooted someplace else in my body. If the gall bladder didn't appear, it would need to be surgically removed. I stayed in that position for two hours waiting for my gall bladder to make its screen debut, but it never did. I was wheeled back to my room to await Dr. Kochman.

In a relatively short period of time Dr. Kochman returned with the test results, having concluded that my gall bladder needed to be surgically removed. I was scheduled for surgery in two days and would be kept on opiates until that time to help me maintain some level of comfort.

Considering where my health stood 24 hours prior to this news, the announcement of gall bladder surgery was a colossal relief. Anything at this point was more manageable than a liver transplant when graduate school was looming in a matter of days.

As plans were being made for surgery, there wasn't anything left for my family to do other than go home, relax, and come back tomorrow knowing that things were being managed. As my mom and Bridget filtered out of the room, Daddy waited to be the last one to leave. He came over to me, began to cry, and wrapped his arms around me. I began to cry as well, not because I was upset at the state of my current fortunes, but because I hated to see Daddy upset. He was the Constant; he wasn't supposed to break down. In that moment I saw the fullness of human emotion and the ties that bind the family together as a living unit of love. I had been through a whirlwind of physical and emotional torment that day and learned much from the experience, but in that moment I let the pain go, and just held onto my Dad. I was proud that he had chosen my shoulder to cry on.

I received a visit from an older-looking doctor the following afternoon. His name, he said, was Dr. Noel Williams, and he would be performing my surgery. He gave me a thorough explanation of the surgery, how long it would take, and what I could expect afterward. Depending on how the gall bladder was removed, recovery time could be anywhere from a couple of days to six weeks. This required more dialogue since I was scheduled to begin classes the following Monday.

Dr. Williams explained that if the surgery was done laparoscopically, recovery time was days; if a larger incision was made, this lengthened the recovery time to six weeks. I voiced my concern over a six-week recovery and strongly encouraged him to push the limit if necessary, in order to perform the surgery laparoscopically. Dr. Williams asked if it was a question of receiving disability from my employer. I explained to him politely that I was scheduled to begin my first year of graduate school on Monday. He stated, "I'll do what I can, but I can't promise anything, and I won't know how it will go until I get in there." Dr. Williams made it clear that my health and the success of the procedure came first.

My personal life was a factor he would consider, but was not willing to compromise my physical soundness for the sake of it. I appreciated his straightforward approach and honesty.

On the day of surgery, I was wheeled down on a gurney, lying flat, to the operating room. For this particular surgery I chose to sport a baby-blue fish-net type shower cap (similar to the one your stereotypical high school lunch lady wore) with matching baby-blue sockettes. Immediately, as the doors to the operating room swung open, the numbing coldness of the room enveloped me like a fog. I was lifted and transferred from the gurney to the operating table, and thankfully, allowed to keep my blanket.

There were people milling about the room walking quickly from one task to another. In the midst of the bone-chilling cold, I shivered beneath my blanket and was suddenly gripped within the breathless fist of a debilitating sense of fear. I responded by blocking everything out. I stared at the ceiling and did what I did best in these scenarios: searched for pleasantries and patterns in the tiles. A doctor appeared above me and in the shadow of the overhead lamp said we would be starting momentarily. With my relationship with God recently repaired, I began praying as quickly as I could, reciting the same reliable prayers I always said when I felt this way, a "Hail Mary" and an "Our Father."

At the close of prayer, the doctor appeared above me once again with a mask in his hand. "Ok, we're going to get started. I'm doctor...[I don't recall his name] and I'm going to place a mask over your mouth. Just breathe normally." The mask was strategically shaped to cover both my nose and mouth. It felt cumbersome and rather intimidating as I exhaled before the mask was placed over my face and drew a breath once it was held in place. Immediately I began coughing uncontrollably, trying frantically to shove the mask from my face when I realized just as quickly that I had been given a paralytic and couldn't move my arms. I began to panic; unable to catch my breath and feeling that things had taken a dark turn, a thousand thoughts scrambled through my mind: Was I allergic to the anesthesia and would be paralyzed but unable to say so? Was I choking and unable to tell the doctor? The heaviness in my lungs felt as though I were drowning in tar. In reality, these thoughts all passed through my state of tortured semi-consciousness in less than three seconds, then it all went black.

I woke up in recovery in an incredible amount of pain with no idea where I was. As I began to fight off the effects of the anesthesia, a nurse appeared. I asked if the doctor had been able to remove my gall bladder laparoscopically. She replied, "Yes." with no further elaboration. Upon hearing the news that the procedure had been successful and still feeling the effects of the anesthesia, I began to cry. My recovery time would be days, not weeks, so I could start classes on Monday. I breathed a huge sigh of relief.

The relief was quickly replaced by the intense pain that I had apparently been able to block out momentarily while I contemplated my educational future. The nurse told me that she had already administered some morphine and that it should become active any second. When I told her that morphine had no effect on me, she wanted to debate me on how I had arrived at that realization, saying that I should just give it time. I was in no mood for a debate and didn't feel like being in pain one second longer. I restated my case, lost, and was given more morphine.

The shot of morphine would hit my system and relieve my pain for a literal minute or two, leaving me with no choice but to call the same nurse and ask for more. Each time I asked, I was denied and told that I could only be dosed every 20 minutes or so. It was horrible. I felt as though the surgery was still taking place, only I was awake. This same process continued for the next two hours: a shot of morphine every 20 minutes, relief for one or two minutes, then continuous agony. Someone from hospital services eventually came and wheeled me back to my room. Relieved to be out of that hell hole, I closed my eyes and tried to rest for a while, despite the pain.

When I first awoke in recovery, I hadn't noticed the two tubes protruding from my body with plastic bulbs on the end. Whatever was slowly filling the bulbs looked terribly gross. My nurse that day was a woman named, Liz. She was about my age, friendly, upbeat, and brightened my room. She explained everything to me in as much detail as I wanted. The tubes in my side were meant to direct the drainage of bodily fluids away from the area where the gall bladder had been removed. Liz also delivered the momentous news that I would only be in the hospital until Saturday (it was Thursday). My recovery would last about a week, so if I took it easy it would be highly feasible that I would have no issues starting classes on Monday. I could have jumped up and planted a huge kiss on Liz for giving me such good news. I looked up at the ceiling and thanked God for seeing me through the surgery and allowing me to start graduate school on time.

The rest of my hospital stay was a blur. My family visited frequently, but for the most part those two days faded away in the half-slumber of being largely confined to bed with doses of opiates. The only thing I remember clearly before being released was the doctor's arrival to remove my drainage tubes. He came in early on Saturday morning, probably around 6:30 a.m. This was not Dr. Williams—I had never before met this guy. He did briefly introduce himself and explained that he would be taking out the drains.

"Ok," I said, "will it hurt?" "No, it will be over before you know it." he assured me. I asked him to let me know when he was about to pull. He said, "Ok, on the count of three. One, two…" and then he pulled the tube from my side without warning. The pain shot through my body like a lightning bolt. It seemed to reach every one of my nerves in record time and for a brief moment absolutely paralyzed me. The whole ordeal probably took less than a few seconds but when the tube was out and I was able to move again, I let the doctor have it full blast. I jumped all over him saying, "Are you kidding me? That hurt like hell. And what happened to three?" He said, "Sorry. I knew it would be over quickly and I thought if I caught you off guard it wouldn't be that bad." I said, "Listen. If I ask if something is going to hurt and it will, you better tell me it will. I don't care if it hurts, I just want the truth so I know what to expect. Is that too much to ask?"

He stammered, "No, and again, I apologize. Is there anything you need?" I thought to myself, "Yeah, a gun to blow your brains out," but just said, "No thanks." and he left. I was surprised at my nerve, to speak to a doctor that way.

Liz released me that afternoon. I was glad I had the chance to say goodbye to her, as it felt like I had known her my entire life. She kept me focused and positive during a time when I thought my life might come crumbling down at any moment.

My parents came to drive me to their house—I wasn't quite ready to fully fend for myself that soon after being discharged and was told by Liz that I would need to make sleeping arrangements for lying on an incline. There was a great amount of tightness around my abdomen from the surgery and I couldn't lie flat without suffering tremendous pain. I thought that night about everything that had transpired over the last few days. I was extraordinarily lucky to have dodged the proverbial bullet once more—that this time around, it was my gall bladder and not my liver. I was grateful to have had a talented surgeon and a nurse like Liz to care for me. I also spent a great deal of time absorbing all that had transpired between me and the rest of my family. The underlying current in all of us was the confluence of love and fear, which periodically produced unpredictable results. It had been a frightening time for each of us. I realized that in the future, I had to do a better job of managing the situation when it came to these episodes as I knew they would increase in gravity and frequency. I couldn't place any further stress on my family by allowing them to walk around believing I could die at any moment. I decided before falling asleep that I needed to protect them from any potentially upsetting fluctuations in my health.

Chapter 9:
Lurking in the Shadows

MY FIRST SEMESTER PASSED quickly in a continuous flurry of classes, exams and projects. It was good, and deeply satisfying, to head home for the holidays. While driving, with little else to do and feeling the spirit and giddiness of the holidays already upon me, I decided to play a little well-intentioned joke on Daddy. As I pulled into the driveway, I called and told him that traffic was awful, and it would be at least three hours before I could get home. I heard the disappointment in his voice as he said, rather softly, "Ok, just take your time and we'll see you when you get here. There'll be a hot plate for you in the microwave." Just then, I hung up the phone and walked in the house as my mom said to him, "Hon, someone just came in..." I heard the sound of the softened leather as he rose from his favorite chair to see who it was, and as he rounded the corner, saw me and said, "Jackass." He grabbed me and embraced me with a hug and kiss. My mom's face was alight when she saw me and walked over with arms open to hug and kiss me as well. It was so good to be home.

After my mom went to bed, Daddy and I went to watch TV until it was time for him to retire as well. We watched Gene Autry and the "Lone Ranger" just as we always did. Pat, Gene's side-kick, handed him a letter from the post and said in a slow, stereotypical southern drawl, "Gene, a letter for you. It's marked urgent." As Pat handed the letter to Gene, I said in imitation, "Hey, Pat! It's your HIV results. I guess we should open it." Daddy was taking a drink at the time, which nearly came through his nose when he started laughing.

Daddy also loved the "Lone Ranger." It involved a series of pretty similar scenarios, with someone in trouble eventually being rescued with the help of the hero and a side-kick. My dad had a magical and innocent way of watching these shows through a child-like lens of simple enjoyment; he was able to allow them to be what they were without the complicated expectations we impose on everything as adults. As I sat there with him, I too was able to adopt a view through that lens and lay aside my anxieties, allowing myself to just be, with my dad, in a quietly comforting space.

The "Lone Ranger" aired following Gene Autry, and Daddy decided to continue the humor we had started earlier. In this particular episode, someone had been shot as the Lone Ranger said to his pal Tonto, "We should go into town to see who's responsible for this." As they rode into town, seeking a spot in which to hide their horses, Daddy imitated the Lone Ranger, saying, "Ok, here's the plan. You dress up as a monkey and I'll be an organ grinder. Then we're sure to get to the bottom of this nonsense." I lost it. I laughed so hard that I had to get up and leave the room to catch my breath. After Daddy went to bed, I was left alone in the dim lamplight of the den and thought to myself, "God, I've missed spending times with him like that."

In typical fashion, the holidays came and passed into memory far too quickly. The next semester would be a different, better than the first, I thought, so long as my energy levels remained steady and I kept in good health.

After two weeks at school, my sister Megan's twins celebrated their first birthday. The twins were born the day following my birthday—I had turned 30. There was a party in town at the local Italian restaurant and it was great fun with tons of pizza and appetizers.

One afternoon before returning to school, Daddy asked if I would help him move the boxes of Christmas decorations out of the basement and into the garage. After making two trips with average-sized, relatively light boxes, Daddy said he needed a minute to rest. He was terribly out of breath and seemed nearly exhausted. I saw at that moment that this wasn't just Daddy getting older, it was something else.

As we continued to move boxes, I was concerned about Daddy for several reasons. First and foremost, I was greatly concerned that he wasn't feeling well. The man rarely got sick, and most certainly never complained when he was. Cal Ripken, Jr. and Bret Favre aren't called "Iron Man" for no reason, they earned it, just as Daddy's nickname was The Constant—he earned it. Seeing him this way was troubling.

I was equally concerned that Daddy refused to visit the doctor on an even relatively routine basis. As a kid, my dad was never allowed to go to the doctor unless he lost a limb or was bleeding so profusely that he turned pale. That was the rule, since doctors were expensive. He carried that mindset into his adult life, and to some degree, we perpetuated it as well. Our insistence that Daddy was The Constant caused him to heartily refuse medical treatment unless the situation was severe. We all felt that he had a reputation to uphold and it was a responsibility that he took seriously. Now as an older adult, I knew I was going to need reinforcements in the battle to get him to seek treatment.

There was only one person in the world to whom my dad never said the word "No," and that was my mom. That evening after Daddy had lost his breath, we continued working in the garage and I excused myself to the bathroom as a means through which to speak privately to my mom. I asked if she had noticed anything wrong with Daddy lately. "No," she said, "Why?" and I told her what had happened with the boxes and how winded he was. I emphasized very strongly to her that I truly felt he needed to see a doctor, and sooner rather than later. She said she would take care of it, and I felt better. She was the only one who possessed the necessary skills to reason with my dad in such a way that he would always listen. We kids sure as hell couldn't penetrate that thick head of his, but she could.

Once back at school, I found out Daddy had in fact agreed to go to the doctor. I was sure that he had made a tremendous fuss but Mommy said he didn't complain or fight at all. That concerned me. I continued to become increasingly concerned as the day of his appointment approached, knowing that Daddy's lack of fighting meant he was really not feeling well. It also meant that he probably should have seen the doctor weeks ago, and only my mom's prodding was able to move him to take action.

I called Daddy the night before his appointment, wished him good luck, and told him to call me as soon as he could following the visit. I was intensely distracted and unable to focus on schoolwork. But, there was really nothing else I could do. I had to wait, though waiting is always the hardest part.

On the day of the appointment, I couldn't wait anymore. I called Daddy at work around the time he was due back from the doctor's. He told me they did a full work-up with blood testing and chest x-rays and would call him in a few days.

Later that afternoon, Daddy called, and told me that the doctor had already called him and asked to see him in his office as soon as possible. My body was instantly incapacitated by fear as I felt my heart sink to the bottoms of my feet. All the strength in my body drained away. My mind began racing and finally shut down from the stress. Daddy was still on the line, and I had to say something. "Well, go and see what he has to say and we'll take it from there." Daddy said in a disheartened voice, "Yep. I'll call you afterward." After we said goodbye, I crawled into bed, emotionally exhausted and mentally vacant, and fell instantly to sleep.

The ring of the phone woke me and I sprang to answer it instinctively without even saying hello. "What'd he say?!" I blurted. There was a shadow, he said, on his lung that needed to be examined by a specialist as soon as possible. He said he pressed the doctor to tell him whether or not it was cancer, but the doctor refused to say a word without first having a biopsy and the opinion of the specialist. "Who is it?" I asked, "Who's the specialist?" He said, "Some doctor in Toms River. I'm going to call tomorrow." After a moment of silence on the phone, I began to cry while Daddy was still on the line. "Hey, it's ok. It's ok." he said, in typical Constant fashion. "Believe me, if it is cancer, I'm going to beat it. Just bring it on; this cancer wants none of me." I appreciated his fortitude, while fully accepting that he was being dishonest for the sake of protecting me and providing me with some sense of security.

When I could speak again, I said, "You damn well better. I never got to meet your father, and I don't want my kids to miss out on meeting you." Daddy's voice began to crack as he said, "Alright, I'll let you go. Try to get some schoolwork done and I'll keep you posted." "Will do." I said. "I love you, Dad." "I love you, too." he said, and that was it.

I let it out after that. I couldn't control it. I was scared shitless that I was going to lose my Dad to this cancer or whatever the doctor had seen. I had visions of Daddy bald and vomiting violently from chemo like in the movie *Dying Young*. I saw him frail and unable to care for himself. I had visions of him lying in a casket, appearing to my red and swollen eyes a hollowed shell of his former self. That night I went to the liquor store, bought a six pack of Bass Ale, and drank them all, alone, in my apartment. I refused to answer the phone or speak to anyone.

That week on Thursday, Daddy called. He told me that it was becoming increasingly difficult to get an appointment in New Jersey with a specialist. I was livid. I'd had enough of my dad's life being potentially in danger due to "scheduling difficulties." I offered to call UPenn and find a specialist there and Daddy agreed. We promptly ended the conversation and I called the 1-800-789-PENN hotline to speak to a referral nurse. The nurse asked if Daddy had been officially diagnosed with cancer, and I explained that the doctor was limited by the x-ray at this point and that there had been no biopsy. The referral nurse was hesitant to send us to an oncologist without an official diagnosis, and so referred us to a thoracic surgeon. There was an entire list of qualified physicians and the most difficult part was choosing one. In order to narrow the list I asked the nurse specific questions such as which doctors might specialize in lung cancer in older males with a history of smoking; which physician has more than five years experience as an attending physician; and which doctor is the head of the department or some other specialized group? My reasoning was simply that I wanted the doctor, male or female, who had the most relevant experience that would be beneficial to my dad. I felt that whomever the doctor, he or she would be exceedingly capable of providing Daddy with the treatment he most needed.

The nurse and I finally settled on a specialist named Dr. Kucharczuk. He was a thoracic surgeon who formed a team of other physicians with a collaborative approach to lung cancer cases. This ensured that each patient would receive the best possible care and based on his credentials, Dr. Kucharczuk sounded like the right person for the job.

Daddy was given an appointment for the following Tuesday, a mere five days away. He was floored at how quickly and how smoothly the process worked. Thinking that I had wielded some kind of magic or that I had a dedicated network of personal connections at the hospital, Daddy gave me way too much credit for introducing him to UPenn. As the news spread throughout the family that Daddy had an upcoming appointment, I began getting phone calls from relatives saying what a great job I did getting him the appointment so quickly. The more I tried to tell everyone that I didn't do anything special, the more the mystique surrounded Daddy's appointment with the perception that I had some sort of "Bat Cave" line right to the doctor's office. Though pretty humorous, it couldn't have been further from the truth. Since I was procedurally well-versed in the HUP system, I knew how to speak to the right departments and therefore take some of the circumnavigation out of the phone system, that's all. I get no preferential treatment from the hospital whatsoever, besides being a long-term, very loyal customer.

The day of Daddy's appointment at UPenn I was scheduled for a finance exam at 4:00 p.m. and foolishly attempted to study and remain patient until I heard an update from Daddy. He called, eventually, and said the doctor concluded from his tests that he did indeed have lung cancer, and that it may have spread to his lymph nodes.

With no consideration for literary appeal or construct, this is a brain dump of what flushed through my mind after Daddy told me he had cancer:

> I need to know what's going to happen. Are you going to be ok? What is the doctor going to do next? Do you have to take medication?

Will you have to go through chemo? When are they going to start treatments? How big is the tumor? Is it a tumor? What can I do? Are you ok? How's Mommy, how's Megan? Is it treatable? Did you ask the doctor about a second opinion? Is it from smoking—*how many times did we ask you to stop smoking— are you happy now*? I want to come down there and kick the shit out of you and throw my arms around you at the same time. Did the doctor say you are going to live? What's going to happen next? Tell me what's going to happen—I need to know what is going to happen! How the hell is this happening! What the hell am I going to do—I don't want to be here, I want to be home. Do you want me to come home I can be home in four hours. To hell with my finance exam, I can be there for you if you need me... why aren't you telling me anything?

Daddy had been speaking to me the entire time as my thoughts were speeding like a train about to de-rail, but I was incapable of processing his words. It was as though he was standing in front of me moving his mouth, but everything streaming from his mouth was gibberish.

I began wailing and crying from a deep and wounded place of incomprehensible fear and sorrow. He told me to pull myself together, as I had that finance exam in a half hour. I gathered myself sufficiently enough to make the executive decision that I could not take the exam. Even had

I pushed through the events of that day and taken it I likely would have failed.

I called my professor in his office and was surprised when he picked up the phone. He seemed skeptical when I told him that my father had just been diagnosed with cancer, but agreed to give me a one-day space of time during which to prepare myself. I called Jay also, to tell him what had just happened. He was very supportive and said he would check in on me that evening.

I lay down and cried, pitifully and hard. I cried as though I were vomiting part of my soul, such was the harshness of my tears as they poured onto the soaking wet couch. I couldn't help but think about how Daddy was feeling, physically and emotionally after receiving such news. I wanted to drive home and hold his hand, tell him I would be there for him, and comfort him in any way I could. I asked God for him to live, or to give me whatever he had. I figured I had a better shot at living since I was younger and could endure more stress to my body. More than anything I just didn't want Daddy to be in pain. My childhood fear of one day losing my parents, more specifically my dad, was now a reality.

After crying and thinking in an endless, tortuous cycle, I fell asleep. Whenever I struggled with too many issues simultaneously, I used sleep as the coping mechanism with which to reset my brain.

I talked to Jay later that night. He was frustrated about the finance exam. He said it was difficult and that people walked out thinking, "What the hell was that?" I hated that. I would study, study, study and the professor would hand out an exam that may well have been written in another language. I figured that I wasn't going to bust my ass studying for it then since it was most likely useless. Jay also asked how Daddy was doing. "I think he's probably ok, for now." I said. "It's just a matter of waiting to see what the doctor says should be the next step." He offered to be there for me in any way he could. Another friend of mine, Big Dave, called that night offering the same sentiments. Their caring and graciousness were tremendously appreciated.

That night I spoke to Daddy on the phone once more to have a detailed discussion about what Dr. Kucharczuk had concluded. They initially ran several tests in order to determine that it was definitely cancer. He then said that Dr. Kucharczuk had decided in conjunction with his team that surgery was the best option in my dad's case. It was felt that the infected space of my dad's lung was too large to be treated with chemo therapy, leaving the removal of part, or all, of the lung the most viable option with the best chance of long-term survival. Mom and Dad agreed to move forward with the surgery.

Chapter 10:
My Hero

DADDY'S SURGERY WAS SCHEDULED during the week I was on spring break which was perfect timing for me as I could be there for Daddy and the family as needed. On the day of Daddy's surgery, he had to register at UPenn by 7:00 a.m., which meant that we had to leave the house by 5:30 a.m. at the latest. When the alarm clock sounded at 4:30 a.m., my hand felt like a sledgehammer when I shut it off. I could feel my heart rate begin to rise before we had even left the house.

I packed my school backpack with some clothes and water since we would be staying in a hotel for a few nights while Daddy recovered in the hospital. I also packed for myself a pocket-sized, grass-green jacketed Bible that oddly enough was handed to me one day on my way home from class during the semester. That Bible was well-used while I was at school, since I certainly wasn't expecting both Daddy and I to require surgery before completing my first year.

As my mom drove, everyone was eerily silent that spring morning as the overnight frost began to slowly dissipate in the face of the rising sun. I can't conceive of what must have been racing through my dad's mind, or the pressure he must have felt to be strong in front of the family. The tension grew as we got closer to the hospital and silence accompanied us like a ghost. No one knew what to say so we all chose to say nothing.

I certainly wasn't expecting party hats and poppers but I thought we would be able to carry on a regular conversation without things spinning emotionally out of control. It was the middle of spring training and the Yankees were getting their team together. We could easily have spent the ride talking about how "we" were going to do it this year as if Daddy, OB and I were on the team—but there was nothing.

At the hospital, my mom and dad registered and took care of preliminaries. Then we sat to wait. The waiting was perhaps the most tortuous part when it seemed that in the crowded room everyone was called before Daddy, as families gave hugs and whispered loving reassurances to one another. I began pacing the room, unable to contain myself in the seat.

As I repeated the motions of sitting, standing and pacing, my thoughts circled like a grindstone: should I tell Daddy I was scared, or nervous, and didn't want to lose him? I would have traded places with him in a heartbeat if given just one chance. I wanted to thank him for all the times he played ball with me, for all the gifts he had ever given me, for giving me strength and courage when I couldn't find those attributes in myself, and apologize for all the times I had ever hurt him or treated him badly. I chose, instead, to say nothing. I felt at the moment of that decision the thoughts begin to poison my mind, seeping into the crevices of every thought that followed until they were interwoven like a labyrinth from which I couldn't escape. The monster within was my burning fear that something might happen to my dad that day, leaving all those thoughts unspoken. Perhaps it was the best choice; Daddy certainly didn't need to witness his 30-year-old son breaking down before his eyes and then be called into surgery.

After Daddy was called to verify his insurance information we were moved to another area. I don't remember waiting long before he was called to change into a hospital gown and lie down on a gurney to be prepared for surgery. Mommy, OB and I were quick to be assured we would see him again before he was taken.

He was dressed in the white HUP hospital gown with which I was quite familiar and a pale blue surgical cap. For the first time, he looked old and frail as he lay on that gurney. It was tough to hold back my tears and make my best effort to be the Constant for him when he needed it.

Mommy and Daddy exchanged some private words as my mom began to cry. OB then stepped in, did an incredible job of comforting my mom and then shared some words with Daddy himself. I waited to have my words with Daddy last, not wanting anyone to be within hearing distance when he and I talked. I know that I said nothing noteworthy, but the words were private and shared only between Daddy and me, which is all that mattered to me at that moment: "You are the toughest man I know. And I don't really give a shit what you have to do between now and the next time I see you, but you better do whatever it takes to be sure that I see you again. Give em' hell." Daddy replied, "Bring it."

He remained the Constant until they came to wheel him away, at which point he began humming "Taps," the song that is played at a traditional military funeral. I smiled and thought, "What a jackass."

The rest of the day was spent trying to find creative ways to pass the time more quickly, of which there are none under those circumstances. The hours dripped by from one minute to the next and one half-hour into an hour. Family members began calling for updates only to hear there were none. After Daddy had been in surgery for about three hours, we received an update that he was tolerating the surgery well, but it would take more time before there would be any substantial conclusions.

Daddy is the second of five kids. He has an older brother, Michael (Uncle Mike), two younger sisters, Margaret Ann (Aunt Marg) and Maureen (Aunt Moe), and a younger brother, Tom (Uncle Tom). All of them were married with children of their own with the exception of Aunt Marg, who is a Roman Catholic nun. In addition to Daddy's brothers and sisters, there was his mother, my grandmother, Nana Bonner. We did our best to keep everyone informed with the most current information.

I don't recall exactly how long Daddy was in surgery, maybe seven hours, but I do remember receiving the call that he was in recovery and that Dr. Kucharczuk was on his way to debrief us on Daddy's status and answer any questions. This concerned me; tensions were high, my family had a million questions, and I didn't want to see the doctor be pummeled immediately upon stepping into the room. I had been through this type of process before and was confident that the doctor would do his best to explain things but would ask that questions be held until the end. When OB took a stack of index cards from his pocket, I cringed inside, but he had every right to ask the doctor as many questions as he felt were appropriate. When Dr. Kucharczuk came into the room, he looked much younger than I had expected to the degree that I had a difficult time believing that a guy who looked to be my age was the authority on lung cancer. However, he was extremely poised, very gracious, and a consummate professional. He introduced himself to each of us by shaking hands and concluded by saying, "It's very nice to meet all of you." I watched his mannerisms intently, and decided finally that he was the real deal.

Dr. Kucharczuk explained that the end goal of the surgery was to remove the portion of Daddy's lung that was housing the tumor as well as the surrounding margins. I came to understand eventually that the margins were the areas surrounding the tumor, in which there were no visible signs of cancer but were at risk for containing traces of cancer that should be removed.

The majority of the tumor was located in the upper portion of Daddy's right lung, but had spread down into the lower portion of the lung due to the tail-like shape of the tumor's growth. I envisioned the tumor looking much like a light bulb with its mass concentrated at the top while narrowing toward the base. They were not able to obtain clean margins during the surgery given how much surface area the tumor covered and were forced to remove Daddy's entire right lung. I could tell that Dr. Kucharczuk was disappointed in the fact that he couldn't save a portion of the lung as he visualized the surgery while speaking to us.

The questions began to rise slowly, such as "When can we see him?" and "How long will he be in the hospital?" Dr. Kucharczuk gave us a thorough overview of what the next few days would entail for Daddy: he would be in the hospital for four or five days and could then go home, though it would be up to two months before he could return to work and several weeks before he could drive.

As the questions gradually became more intense, I appreciated Dr. Kucharczuk's willingness to answer each one with as much knowledge and attention to detail as he could. The questions generally focused on Daddy's long-term prognosis and whether or not he would require chemotherapy. We asked if he would need a ventilator, or be able to breathe freely with one lung. The most painful question was how long Daddy might have to live. Despite the painful nature of our session with Dr. Kucharczuk, I was very proud of everyone in my family for asking such intelligent questions at the right moment.

When we finally saw Daddy, his arms were bruised from his biceps to his wrists, while tubes and wires protruded from his abdomen and chest. He was attached to a breathing monitor, which filled me with a sense of dread as though he were being kept alive by artificial means and might not awaken. I was afraid to touch him at first, until a nurse came into the room. He awoke, and was responsive. My entire being embraced the shock of enthusiasm that resonated

within me at seeing Daddy alive once more after the battle
he had just endured.

We each had a chance to talk to Daddy for a few
moments, who drifted in and out of consciousness as he
was lulled to sleep by the remnants of the anesthesia and
medications for pain. As we were about to leave, the nurse
returned to check on Daddy one more time. Daddy opened
his eyes as wide as he was able to and seemed to be coherent
while he asked what had happened. The nurse very kindly
replied that he had just returned from surgery after having
his lung removed. With a rock-solid, stern face and a loud,
abrupt voice my dad said, "What!? I didn't come in here
to have my lung taken out, I was here for problems with
my knee!" The nurse's face was priceless. After a few tense
moments Daddy said, "I'm only kidding." then instantly
fell asleep.

We all stayed in the Penn Towers Hotel that evening,
feeling far better at the conclusion than we had at the
beginning of the day. I climbed into bed at only 8:30 p.m.
and fell fast asleep in the room I was sharing with OB and
his girlfriend, Jennie.

The next morning we all headed to the hospital early,
all wanting to spend an equal amount of time with Daddy.
Aunt Marg, Aunt Moe and Nana Bonner were on their way
to visit as well. Somehow, I managed to become separated
from the group and was on my own wandering through the
hospital floors. It isn't a surprise, really; I normally seek
out ways to be alone during periods of crisis or tremendous
tension. Eventually, I found my way to Daddy's room,

extremely nervous about how he would look the day after. I girded myself for the image of walking into the room with Nana Bonner weeping over Daddy's bruises and tubes while trying my best to stay strong under the pressure.

I turned the corner at the far end of the hallway that led to Daddy's room, and could see people through the doorway sitting, but looking up. I saw something that caused my blood pressure to plummet and the muscles in my legs to lose their strength. As Nana Bonner sat in the first seat closest to the door, I saw her reach out her hand and from the other side of the doorway, Daddy walked toward her to take the seat adjacent to hers. To this day I am surprised that the shock of that sight didn't cause me to faint. I stopped in the hallway, unable to move or divert my eyes as they gazed in wonder at Dad's tenacity and fighting spirit. I began to cry as the emotions of thanks and relief washed over me first like a crashing wave and then gently, as if I were being cradled in the purity of my love for my father. To see him standing within 24 hours of having a lung removed was, to me, a miracle. I looked up to the sky and whispered, "Thank you." took a deep breath, composed myself, and walked in to see Daddy. My soul was full, and as I crossed the threshold into that small space I felt as though I radiated light throughout the entire room.

I gave Nana Bonner a kiss and nonchalantly walked over to Daddy, gave him a kiss, and asked, "How ya doin?" "Doing good, doing good," he replied. I don't know how I held back the emotions but somehow I did. I learned from the Constant himself that although I may not feel strong inside, I always looked strong on the outside.

Daddy's room quickly began to fill with visitors, so I willingly relinquished my visitor's pass to give others some time. Although the greater part of me wanted fiercely to stay by his side, I felt confident that my relationship with him was strong enough that I didn't need to be physically near him in order for him to know that I was there—just as I consistently felt that he was with me, regardless of the circumstances.

There has never been a day in history wherein a son felt more proud of his father than I did that day, watching Daddy walk around his hospital room, speak to others, smile and crack jokes. The love and the pride I felt for him were indescribable.

Having recently patched up my relationship with God, I owed Him a tremendous amount of thanks for letting Daddy stay with us a while longer. Once more I felt that God had been there the whole time.

After some time, OB and I went back up to see Daddy. We didn't expect to find him awake, or alone, but he was. He asked to go for a walk, and after clearing it with the nurse away we went. After we had walked far enough out of hearing distance from the nurse's station, Daddy said, "You know, this really sucks." Instantly I was filled with compassion for my father, who had just undergone such a long, trying ordeal and fought back my emotions. OB asked calmly, "Well, what's the matter? Do you feel ok?" As I continued to worry, Daddy said a touch too loudly, "I'm ok...but this is the first time in my 54 years on this planet that I've had to stay in the hospital. It just figures I have a fucking MALE nurse, Steve, to look after me." OB and I cracked up. As funny and fleeting as the moment was, it was a moment we all definitely needed.

Daddy continued to improve over the next few days and was released the following week. After six weeks, he returned to work. His surgical scar was consistently painful: it looked as though a shark had torn into him beneath his armpit leaving a curvature in the shape of a "U" that extended from his back to his chest. We told him to request a pain killer from the doctor but he refused. God forbid the Constant should need pain meds.

It seemed now that the worst was behind us. Daddy was back; we breathed a collective sigh of relief with Daddy at the head of our family pack. The news of Daddy's cancer had shaken my family to its core, but now we felt able to once again look toward a bright future.

Within three months of the surgery, Daddy began experiencing frightening episodes of breathlessness. He could be sitting, walking, standing, eating, drinking or even sleeping—it could strike at any time, forcing him to stop what he was doing to focus exclusively on his breathing. It was obvious that he labored with each breath he drew; the car was always kept ready should a true emergency arise.

We did on one occasion rush him to the hospital, when he was unable to draw a breath for an inordinate amount of time. He was medicated and began to breathe normally, but it scared the shit out of us. Other than an inhaler to help relieve any constriction in his passageways, the doctors didn't do much else for him. This frustrated the hell out of me since I felt the issue was very basic: Daddy could not, of his own volition, get enough oxygen into his system, and therefore into his brain. He didn't need an asthma-type drug for airway constriction, he needed oxygen—just air. Why give him an inhaler rather than an oxygen tank? I was forced to trust what the doctors decided was the best plan of action for Daddy, since I was versed only in issues with the digestive system and liver.

One evening our family went to a party, just hours after Daddy had been released from the hospital following a lack of breathing episode. As I sat, scanning the room for other members of my family, I saw Mommy sitting next to Daddy, while OB chatted with Uncle Tom. Bridget and Megan were talking in another area. I turned my attention to Daddy, and could see on his face the worn look of a brave, tired man. I wanted him to be home, resting quietly until he felt ready to take on the world once more. People milled about the room, chatting and having a pleasant time. They stopped to ask Daddy how he was feeling, and he assured everyone that he was fine. I don't know to this day whether he really was or not.

I continued to stare at Daddy, wishing I could hold him, wishing I could nurse him back to health or that he could draw from me as much strength and energy as he needed. If only such things were possible. I loved him more than anything, and would do anything for him. At one point he caught me staring, and saluted just like he did when we were kids. He would either smoothly glide his palms across the table, or click his heels and say, "I'm the Constant, that's all, just the Constant." With welling pride, I smiled

127

and saluted back. The times of teasing Daddy about being the Constant with comments like "Get the hell out of here!" were pretty much gone. Though those moments were all said from a loving place, we were too thankful now just to have Daddy still with us to tease or take him for granted. The guy was more than the Constant: he was a hero, he was my best friend, and he was Dad, my dad.

Chapter 11:
Don't Ever Give Up

THINGS WERE LOOKING UP for me when I returned to school that August. While Daddy continued to suffer lack of breathing episodes, he always bounced back. He regained much of his strength and even golfed on a few occasions. I had also talked to Sue several times over the summer and got her to agree to visit me before classes started.

On the day she was due to arrive, I paced my apartment, walking repeatedly outside to check my cell phone for any missed calls. When she pulled in front of the apartment complex, I jumped in her car and showed her where to park. After we parked, I threw my arms around her and gave her an affectionately tight squeeze, never wanting to let go. God, I missed her.

Once her things were in the apartment we did what we did best—talked. We talked like a couple of school girls. At some point we must have eaten something and I may even have introduced her to Jay, Big Dave, and Jay's girlfriend, Beth, though I have no recollection of when that took place. That night, as we lay in bed, I draped my arm over her waist and could feel the heat emanate through her pajamas. It was August and hot as hell, but I didn't care. Being next to Sue aroused feelings of love and security in me and the safety I had felt as a child. I slept better that night than I had in a very long time.

Sue's time with me was over far too soon and saying goodbye was always extremely taxing. Amid the hugs, kisses and tears there was a subconscious agreement that we were fully "together," though no verbal stamp was placed on it. We made plans to talk more and try to visit more often. We both knew that being on different continents would present a challenge, but we were willing to try. With one year of graduate school down and one more to go, I would have plenty to keep me busy. Sue was busy as well with moving her business unit from London to Dublin.

My health, and more specifically my liver numbers, also kept me busy. I was having blood work done regularly and being monitored more closely since the discovery of a spike in my liver enzymes—my AST and ALT levels had increased. I didn't know much about AST and ALT; all I knew was that they were the two liver enzymes around which the monitoring of my condition was focused. The numbers had increased from around 120 to 180. "Whatever," I thought, "I don't feel any different so I'm sure I must be fine." The doctors thought differently. I was ordered to have blood drawn every month to ensure that things weren't progressing more quickly than anticipated. If you saw me on the street, you never would guess there was anything wrong with me; I continued to lift weights and even run when I found time. However, on paper I was a different story.

Maintaining balance that semester was trying, at best. I kept tabs on Daddy, in addition to Mommy's mother Nana Pawlowski, who'd had back surgery that November, not to mention my own supposedly declining health. At the conclusion, I stood back and was amazed at the ferocity of my determination. I had successfully fought my way through another semester, and was now looking forward to Christmas.

The whole family eagerly awaited Christmas that year—and we certainly had much for which to be thankful. Daddy, even by that Christmas, continued to have breathing episodes, though overall he appeared to be doing well. I had made plans to spend New Year's in Dublin with Sue, and was counting down the days until we would be together.

Our Christmas tradition consisted of attending mass at 4:00 p.m. on Christmas Eve, then celebrating the holiday meal out at a restaurant. After dinner, we all piled back to Mommy and Daddy's and exchanged gifts. The sheer mass of boxes and bags under the tree that year looked like a Christmas miracle, the type of scene from happily-ending feel-good classic Christmas films. There was a three-foot wall of gifts, completely surrounding the lower portion of the tree and rising to the second row of branches. It was truly a magical sight as the lights twinkled down and reflected off the wrapped boxes, multiplying the glow of each by a thousand. I was transported back to the years when Santa was real, and the anticipation of Christmas grew with each passing day. As the camera shutters snapped and wrapping paper was joyfully torn asunder, I sat quietly and soaked it all in. That Christmas still shines brightly in my mind as one that I will treasure for the rest of my life.

Two days following Christmas, I excitedly boarded a plane to Ireland to be with Sue. We talked and laughed for hours on end, and in between had drinks at the Ice Bar, made potato skin appetizers, ate my famous ziti and took day trips. In typical fashion, the inevitable farewell ripped my heart from my still bleeding chest.

Once I returned home, I was depressed. Having Sue on the other side of the ocean—the woman whom I loved more than anything in the world—was achingly frustrating.

I headed back to school almost immediately after coming home. Jay, Big Dave and I decided that we should go away for spring break as a gift to ourselves for making it through the MBA program. It was a novelty—none of us had ever vacationed away for spring break during our undergrad years, as none of us could have afforded it. We were older now, had some money, and settled on taking a cruise in the Caribbean.

Classes slowed about two weeks before leaving for spring break so I took the opportunity to visit with everyone at Mommy and Daddy's house. Nana Bonner and Aunt Moe were also going to visit Daddy and check on his health. That Saturday morning, Daddy and I drove to the supermarket. Although he insisted he was fine, and indeed appeared to be so, I wasn't comfortable letting him do any heavy lifting. We listened to a CD in the car that he had mixed for himself, which wasn't all that bad. Let's just say Clint Eastwood is a better actor/director than country music singer. Daddy's favorite song was a rendition of the "William Tell Overture," which also happened to be the theme song for the "Lone Ranger." I smiled as he conducted in the car as we drove, and asked him to turn it up, which he gladly obliged.

When we were home from the store and had put the last

bag of groceries away, Daddy struck up a conversation with me that sucker-punched a hole through my cautious optimism for his health. No one else was around, and I'm not sure why, but I was glad they weren't. It gave me the opportunity to talk with Daddy the way we were most comfortable, which may not have made too much sense to others. He told me that the breathing issues were still frequent, and were in fact growing worse. He described what it felt like, the violent loss of breath, and having to pause everything to focus on drawing one more breath, then another, and still another. "I really don't think I'm going to make it through one of these times." he said. I became explosively angry. I was angry at the fact that he was faced with this situation, and most of all, angry that if Daddy was telling me, it was true and not an exaggeration. I wasn't sure what to say, or what to do. Rather than blowing up, however, in spite of my feelings, here's a paraphrased synopsis of what I chose to say:

> When it comes to being sick, there are definitely peaks and valleys. The peaks are great and the valleys suck. When you hit a valley, you will most likely visit the darkest and loneliest place in which you've ever had the misfortune of being. It's at that point that you need to reach out to somebody, whether it be me, Mommy, Ownie, or someone else inside or outside the family. Reach out to them and let them know what you're going through; whatever you do, don't go through it alone. I've gone through it; not to the extent that you have, but I've been to those dark and lonely places and I needed other people to help me climb out—you were

the person I relied on most. Facing an illness alone makes it very easy to give up—and I don't want you to ever give up. I want you around for as long as possible. I never met your father and I don't want my kids to go through that. So talk to the doctor and tell him that you can't breathe; tell him you need an oxygen tank, and see what he says. That stupid, fucking nebulizer doesn't do shit. But promise me, promise me that if you do ever feel like giving up, you'll call me. I will be right there for you every step of the way—but please, Dad, don't ever, ever give up.

After I had finished, he simply said, "I promise I'll do my best." With that the conversation drew to a close and the day wore on.

The rest of the weekend was great. It was an awesome time with Aunt Moe, Nana, Megan and her kids. We broke out "Karaoke Revolution" with Daddy choosing to sing "Celebration" by Kool & the Gang, but he was booed off stage. OB filmed the whole thing, which was hysterical. As Daddy sang, he was reading the feedback from the game aloud, with choice scores such as "Awful" and "Poor." We laughed so hard I truly thought Nana Bonner would wet herself. It was a great, great, day.

I went back to school looking forward to the cruise the following weekend. When it finally arrived, we packed the car and began driving when I realized the directions we had from Penn State to the port in D.C. were just bad; it would take us an egregiously long time to get there. I called Daddy, hoping he might know a better way, and as we talked, it was obvious that he was completely preoccupied with Megan's kids—he couldn't get enough of playing with them. He also didn't know another way to get to D.C., so I just smiled, knowing that he hadn't really thought about it, considering he never stopped playing with the kids the entire time we spoke. I told him I'd call him when we got back.

While on the cruise, we made a habit of going to the club each night for drink specials, and to try and meet people our own age. I certainly wasn't looking for a girl to hook up with since I was with Sue, but Big Dave and Jeremy, Jay's brother, were scoping for girls. We usually left the club around three or four o'clock in the morning, slept for a while, then went about starting the day. I bought a phone card and made a point of calling Sue from each island. There was no way I could go a week without speaking to her.

One night, Big Dave, Jeremy, and I went down to the club as we normally did. I had a drink or two, but didn't feel much like hanging around. Physically, I felt fine, but something else tugged at me—a feeling somewhere deep within myself that things were not right in the universe and that there was nothing I could do about it. I headed back to my room. Big Dave and Jeremy wondered what was wrong and why I was leaving, but I just had no heart to stay.

Up on the deck of the ship, the sky over the waters was black, lit only by the pallid moonlight. I felt down as I stared as deeply as my human eyes would allow below the surface of the ocean, wondering what secrets were kept there and if they ever would be discovered. I wasn't convinced I would want to know them all if they were. There was a slightly malicious touch to the air as it swept me from side to side, shoving and pushing me, forcing upon me the feeling that I was insignificant and small...that life could be taken from me, suddenly and without warning or regret. An entire world lay beyond the horizon I could not discern that dark night, filled with people going about their daily business and living life. I wondered what the future held for me—or if I had a future. Would this liver thing finally catch up with me? What about Daddy? Feeling dejected, I walked slowly and purposelessly back to my room to try calling Sue.

As I lay on the bed talking to Sue, she asked if I was all right. She knew. She knew me better than anyone. "I just needed to talk to you." I said. I insisted that she take down the information to reach the ship, should she need to speak to me. I was having a good time, I told her, but I missed her tremendously, and loved her. Something was wrong—though neither of us had any idea what it was.

At some point during the night, Big Dave came back to the room and went to sleep. He snored like a hibernating bear and as I rolled over to tell him to shut up, the phone rang before the words could exit my mouth. I lay frozen in the bed suddenly overcome by a tremendous feeling of dread. Reluctantly, I walked over to the phone and picked it up. It was Sue. "I need to talk to you, Honey."

Softly, she said, "It's your dad..."

My Mom and Dad's wedding photo in November 1970 (above). Courtesy of Marilyn and Owen Bonner

Ownie, me, and Bridget posing at the Scirabba's backyard fence in Toms River, NJ, in the fall of 1976 (left). Courtesy of Marilyn Bonner

Ownie, me, Bridget, and Megan in our house in Bayonne, NJ, in 1981 (estimated). I would have been 8-years old at the time (above) Courtesy of Marilyn Bonner

*John after his first
liver transplant (left).
Courtesy of Joann
Scirabba*

The Scirabbas were our
next door neighbors in
Toms River that became
family. John and I both
had ulcerative colitis,
primary Schlerosing
Cholangitis, and liver
transplants. John passed
away in 1994 but will
never be forgotten. The
entire Scirabba family
and the memory of John
helped me throughout
my transplant
experience. I love them
all very much.

*Uncle Pete and Aunt Joann
(above). Courtesy of
Joann Scirabba*

*From left to right along
the top row: Mary Jo's
husband, Derek Perry,
John and Peter. Sitting
in the front row are
Mary Jo, Amy, and
Amy's husband, Drew
Martin (left). Courtesy
of Joann Scirabba*

This is a picture of me at 12-years old in 1985. I'm sitting on the same radiator Megan severely burned her hand on years earlier (left). Courtesy of Marilyn Bonner

These are my two most favorite pictures of Daddy and I. This picture was taken in front of Nana Bonner's house with Daddy in a suit and me in my Sunday best. I supported the same Bonner ears Daddy had when he was a kid (above). Courtesy of Megan Lang

Sharing a love for baseball, it was a dream-come-true that I could visit the National Baseball Hall of Fame with Daddy in Cooperstown, New York. As I got older, I looked more and more like Daddy, still supporting the same Bonner ears (above).
Courtesy of Marilyn Bonner

Sue and I at a friend's wedding in February of 2004 (above).
Courtesy of Patricia Olsem

Me with the Donnelly family at a birthday party for Sue's mom in 2007. Standing along the back row from left to right are Sue's brother-in-law and sister, Steve and Nancy Westington, Sue, Sue's parents, Vince and Claire Donnelly, Sue's sister, Janet Donnelly, Sue's brother, Kevin Donnelly, and Sue's brother-in-law, Bob Burgee. In the front row are Sue's nieces, Tara and Kailey Westington (above). Courtesy of J. J. Donnelly Photography

This is the obituary photo that ran in the paper after Daddy died on March 13, 2004 (above). Courtesy of Owen Bonner (OB)

Daddy was noticeably absent from my graduation from Pennsylvania State University after earning my MBA in May, 2004 (below). From left to right are OB, Bridget, me, Megan, and Mommy. I was wearing one of Daddy's ties in memory of him. Courtesy of Michael Bonner

By Christmas of 2004, I had lost a lot of weight, was visibly jaundiced, itchy all over, and desperately trying to get listed for transplant (left). Courtesy of Susan Donnelly

This picture was taken in mine and Sue's apartment in early January, 2005. I was wearing a sweatshirt I bought for Sue while I was at Penn State. It was one of the only pieces of clothing we had that fit me at a size medium. I hadn't been a size medium since sophomore year of high school (right). Courtesy of Susan Donnelly

This picture was taken of me on my 32nd birthday, January 23, 2005. I was officially listed for transplant five days later (above). Courtesy of Megan Lang

This picture was the last picture taken of me before I was transplanted. Sue and I went to Aunt Moe's house to meet Kimberly for the first time. I had been on the transplant waiting list for over a month and came to the conclusion that I wasn't going to live long enough to be transplanted. I fully expected this to be the last time I saw my family. I was very fortunate to have received my transplant two weeks later (above). Courtesy of Tom Bonner

I first met Liz Ryan when I had my gall bladder removed in August of 2002. Today, Liz is a dear friend, an excellent nurse, and the person who wrote the foreword for this book (left). Courtesy of Liz Ryan

Patti Pfeiffenberger has been my post-transplant coordinator for over six years. She is an incredible transplant nurse who is loved by all transplant patients. I can't thank her enough for the amount of care and attention she gives me on an ongoing basis (right). Courtesy of Patti Pfeiffenberger

Rebecca Farrell was my first post-transplant coordinator who had to deliver some difficult news to me more than once. Her unique ability to empathize with patients is one of her many endearing qualities. I owe her many thanks and then many more (left). Courtesy of Rebecca Farrell

I first met Betsy Knight, a nurse practitioner, while in the hospital after my transplant. She has a million dollar smile that warmed my insides at some of my lowest points ever. She is one of my favorite people in the world as her dedication to patients is unyielding. Photo not available at time of printing.

My Mom,
Marilyn Bonner
(below). Courtesy of
Marilyn Bonner

OB with his family, wife, Jennie, and
kids, little Ownie and baby Sophia
(below). Courtesy of Owen Bonner

Even today, my immediate family helps me out whenever I
need it. They are the people who I love dearly, who I thank
immensely, and who I am most proud to be related to.

Bridget with her family, husband,
Jarlath, and kids, Ryan, Liam,
and Aidan (above). Courtesy of
Bridget Lynch

Megan with her family,
Kieran, Collin, and
Kayleigh (above).
Courtesy of Megan Lang

My beautiful girl, Susie, who is the rock of my strength. I
wouldn't have made it without Sue's continuous love and support.
She has taught me many things about life but most important,
how to love myself. For that, and a million other reasons, I love
her with everything that I am and ever will be (above).
Courtesy of Dan Bonner

Chapter 12:
I'll See You Soon

My MIND BEGAN TO spin uncontrollably. I could hear Sue talking but couldn't understand what she was saying as my mind refused to listen to any of this. She repeated herself several times to no avail as I became increasingly irate. Basically, she said that Megan had called to tell her that Daddy had had another breathing episode, this time losing consciousness. He was revived, but that's all Sue knew. My voice rose and I began yelling, "Is he alive?" "Is he alive?" with growing desperation as Sue's replies became softer. "I don't know, Honey....I'm not sure."

I immediately began to yell, "No, no, no, no, no! Fuck this. This is fucking bullshit. Who did you talk to and how do they know what's going on?" Sue very calmly replied that she had spoken to Megan.

Sue said she would have Megan call my room, after telling me she loved me and was there for me no matter what. I knew I was definitely going to need all she could give.

My heart pounded in my chest as I paced the floor of the room waiting for Megan to ring. The anger and frustration of not knowing what was happening with Daddy grew with each passing second. In no time I was filled with a fury the strength of a tornado—I wanted to punch walls, break everything in my path, fight someone—anything to rid myself of the nauseating feeling that had reached the depths of my being. Megan finally called, distraught, and I asked her to tell me, as calmly as she could, exactly what happened.

Daddy had been struck by a sudden lack of breathing in the middle of the night. He walked downstairs to use his nebulizer, but even that was not able to restore him. He called out for my mom, who ran downstairs to find him clutching the kitchen counter, struggling to draw even the smallest breath of air. She immediately called 911, and an ambulance was sent, but before the police could arrive, Daddy began to collapse. He turned to my mother, saying, "I'm not going to make this one. Tell everyone that I love them." and fell to the floor.

The police began doing CPR, but after 15 minutes were still unable to revive him. My mom was on the phone with Megan while the police worked on Daddy, and asked if they should stop. Megan said to keep trying. They did, and were finally able to secure a low pulse, though by this time Daddy had been unconscious for more than 20 minutes.

I somehow managed to ask if Daddy was alive to which Megan replied something to the effect of his being technically alive, but not conscious. It didn't look like he would wake up.

I woke up Big Dave, who was still half-asleep and drunk. In an instant he pulled himself together and threw his arms around me while I crumbled, using his body to prop up my own as I cried. My next thought was that I had to get home—but the problem was how, from the middle of the ocean.

Dave helped me pack, then I beat on Jay's door until he answered. Jay also threw his arms around me, and I felt extremely fortunate to be surrounded by people who genuinely cared. I said goodbye, and headed out to the customer service area. To the best of my knowledge, there was only one person on board the ship who was capable of helping me get home.

I needed transportation to the airport, then a flight to the Dominican Republic, and finally a flight to Newark, NJ. What happened next completely shocked and appalled me.

The representative told me that he could get me a taxi to the airport, as well as a flight to the Dominican Republic, but that there were no open seats on flights to Newark. I told him as calmly as I could that that was simply impossible and that I was prepared to pay as much as necessary to get to Newark. He wouldn't budge. After debating back and forth about this for several minutes, trying to be very polite, I'd had enough. Without warning, I exploded. The f-bombs fell like rain: "Don't fucking tell me that there aren't any flights to Newark or that there's no fucking seats on any of the planes. It's fucking 7:00 a.m. on a Friday. So, either you don't know what the fuck you're talking about or you don't fucking care." I was in a rage like never before. All I could think of was picking up a car and crushing this guy with it had there been a car within reach. I had never before witnessed such a lack of compassion.

Put off by my indignity and waterfall of profanity, the guy went back to his room to check flights, came out and said, "I can get you to the Dominican Republic and then you're on your own." "Fine." I said, grabbed my itinerary, and was gone.

I caught a cab to the airport near the ship and arrived at the St. Kitts airport shortly thereafter. I called Sue at work since it was now the middle of the day in her part of the world. I debriefed her on what had really happened with Daddy and related my ire at the cruise line's lack of professionalism. Sue offered to help in any way she could, and began looking into flights to Newark as well as a car service that would bring me home. I thanked her up and down and said I would call her from the Dominican Republic.

The flight from St. Kitts was on a dual propeller plane that held 20 people at most, including the pilots and crew. I would be lying if I said I wasn't scared to step on that plane but I had more pressing issues to worry about. I sat and thought about Daddy the whole flight. Tears streamed down my cheeks as I wondered if he was in pain, if he was scared, or if he was aware of anything at all. I felt that I had been rendered helpless; the lack of knowledge concerning Dad's state, and the fact that I wasn't there with him tortured me, tearing gaping holes in my heart. I comforted myself by remembering that Daddy and I had a great relationship, one that could and would transcend the darkness that currently enshrouded me. I hoped he knew I was on my way. By the end of my interior monologue, I had convinced myself that my sole mission was to bring Daddy back, from wherever he was. I whispered out loud, "Hang in there; I'll see you soon."

When I finally arrived in the Dominican Republic, I immediately called Sue. She gave me a list of flights and carriers to Newark. "That fucking asshole from the cruise line had no fucking clue what was going on." I thought to myself.

There were three airlines that ran flights into Newark. I walked to each counter and asked if there were any seats available on their next available flight. The first carrier could put me on standby; I said I'd get back to them if the other carriers couldn't come through. The second carrier had a flight, but it wasn't leaving for several hours. The last carrier was Continental. They had an open seat immediately available and I jumped on it, waiting to hear that it would cost me some egregious sum. Ultimately, I didn't care how much it cost, but I also didn't want the airline to take advantage of me. The total cost was less than $300.00. I felt such gratitude for the airline and the guy at the counter who helped me that I began to cry. I shook his hand and said, "Thank you so much." and made my way over to the boarding area.

I called Sue on the way and told her how fortunate I was to have gotten the flight so quickly and how furious I was with the management of the cruise line. My only problem now was getting from the airport to my parents' house. Sue suggested I call Uncle Andy, my Aunt Moe's husband. He was on top of arranging a limo service to pick me up from the airport and take me home and guaranteed that there would be a ride for me at the airport even if he couldn't secure a limo. With my transportation plans in place, I was free to focus on my goal: Daddy.

I focused all the energy I could muster on bringing Daddy back. My mind was feverish—I knew I could bring him back—I just knew it. He wasn't going to die, I told myself. He's waiting there, in the hospital, for me to pull him through. By the time I landed in Newark, I had convinced myself of this and no one could tell me otherwise.

When I arrived, I found Uncle Tom and Aunt Marg waiting for me, much to my dismay. This meant that I would have to temporarily detour my focus on Daddy in the name of politeness—and I didn't want to. After an exchange of embraces, Uncle Tom said to me, "Dan, we need to talk." I replied, shortly, "Not now, Uncle Tom. I came here to bring Daddy back and that's all I want to focus on." Aunt Marg and Uncle Tom exchanged glances. I knew then that I had been delusional thinking that I would whisk into the room like a hero and make it all ok.

No words passed between us as I waited for my luggage. When the bags arrived I asked Uncle Tom where he had parked and we headed toward the car. Once more, Uncle Tom said, "Danny, we really need to talk." this time a little more forcefully. I wanted no part of the conversation. I wanted to focus on Daddy and only Daddy. However, I knew Uncle Tom had information I didn't have, which was most likely information I needed whether it be good, bad, or indifferent.

Uncle Tom then gave me a full update. Once the police were able to get a pulse on Daddy, he was taken to the hospital and sent directly to the intensive care unit. Daddy's system had suffered for far too long without oxygen, and the doctors were concerned he had sustained irreversible brain damage. He was unconscious and unresponsive. They estimated that Daddy was functioning at a brain capacity level of less than 5%.

I asked Uncle Tom directly if they thought Daddy would make it through this. I don't recall whether he said, "It doesn't look good," or "It doesn't look like he will." but I got the point. I knew then that I had failed at saving Daddy before even getting a chance to try. At once my world was obliterated and I couldn't hold back the waterfall of anguish that washed over me. I was drowning.

Prior to that day I hadn't felt especially comfortable letting foul language fly around Uncle Tom and Aunt Marg, but she was wise, and it was apparent that I was trying too hard to control my emotions. She assured me that she'd heard plenty of foul language from plenty of people, and to go ahead and let it out.

F-bomb after F-bomb fell from my mouth as easily as any word I had ever spoken. I was furious, depressed, empty, terrified, lonely, confused and worried simultaneously. This can't be happening. Daddy really is all right—he has to be. I spoke to him just last week before leaving for the cruise. He was playing with the kids. How in God's name could it have come to this? Uncle Tom and Aunt Marg conveyed that they were feeling the same emotions I was feeling which provided a temporary comfort to me.

By the time we reached the hospital, I was emotionally and physically exhausted. I had been traveling non-stop and had had only a few hours of sleep the previous night. While trying to find Daddy's room, a security officer abruptly stopped me at the elevator and said, "Where do you think you're going?" Already in a volatile state of mind, I reached out to grab the guy as I thought, "Mr. Fucking Tough Guy, huh?" Before I could get my hands on him, another officer quickly interjected, "He's got someone on two." The first guard stepped aside and politely said, "Sorry. Please go ahead." After my initial desire to choke that guard into oblivion, I realized that patients "on two" were those whose fate was already sealed and it was just a matter of time.

I specifically told Uncle Tom that I wanted to spend time with Daddy alone and to please, please not let anyone into the room with me, especially OB, who had a history of taking over in stressful situations. I just wanted some quiet time with Daddy—just the two of us. Not knowing what the next few hours would hold, I was viciously possessive of what little time I was allotted to see him. Uncle Tom agreed and I took the first step toward the double doors that led to Daddy's room.

My feet felt weighed down with lead and I felt entirely unsure of my composure. My body was weak as I neared his doorway, though my spirit and love for him drove me onward. My self-image was jaggedly fractured as my heavy steps carried me to the door; part of me wanted to run away and close my eyes to make this all disappear, while the other half stood a grown man, willing to do anything to be by my father's side. I hesitated at the door. It almost didn't seem real. If anything, I had always wanted to die before Daddy, just so I would never have to witness his death. I summoned every ounce of courage I'd ever had to grip onto the door handle and walked into the room.

Daddy lay on the bed, connected to a respirator. His tongue hung from his mouth and was obviously dry. He was surrounded by tubes and various monitors. His chest rose and fell, and his color was relatively normal. If I imagined hard enough he almost looked as though he was simply sleeping. I touched his hand, which was warm, and said, "Hey, it's me. I'm here for you now, so you just tell me what you need and I'll do it. I know you can't talk, but just give me a sign."

Within a few moments, OB walked in. Furious is the mildest word choice for how I felt. My eyes were ready to shoot flames and scorch every inch of OB's body. He walked over and hugged me, saying, "We'll get through this together." His sentiments were sincere, thoughtful and appreciated. However, I still wanted to spend time with Daddy alone. Not wanting a confrontation, OB and I stayed with him together.

After a while, my exhaustion caught up with me and I had to lie down. As I left to try and rest in the waiting room, OB played some of Daddy's favorite CD's, hoping the familiarity would bring him back to us. I stepped out of the room, tears streaming down my cheeks.

I hadn't slept for long when I woke suddenly, feeling gripped by an unquenchable, nearly frantic desire to have an update on Daddy's condition. I was told that we could do nothing but wait. Until the doctor arrived, no one was in a qualified position to give us news, or the lack thereof. While waiting, and since sleep was out of the question, I returned to Daddy's bedside. My most concerted efforts to make him laugh, move, speak, or even open his eyes were unsuccessful. All I wanted was a sign—any type of sign, a loud breath, a blink of his eyes—anything to let me know that he was still there but unable to vocalize his awareness. There was none.

The doctor explained once he arrived that he would evaluate Daddy and give us all a full report. I followed him to Daddy's room, but was directed to stand outside while Daddy was examined. He clapped his hands repeatedly, called out Dad's name several times loudly and looked for any reaction on the array of monitors. When he emerged, the doctor asked to speak with only immediate family.

Most likely, the doctor explained, Daddy had sustained acute and irreversible brain damage from the prolonged lack of oxygen the night he collapsed. The brains of some, he continued, act in a way that is similar to a computer when it freezes and will "reboot," thereby resetting the body's system and resuming normal activity. There is no medical explanation for why this occurs for some, and not for others who remain unconscious. As my family and I listened to the doctor, my mind raced with questions that seemed trivial and desperate. The chance of Daddy recovering, in his current state, the doctor said, was less than half of one percent. He would most likely never respond to people, sounds, his name, or any other form of stimulus. His physical body would be kept alive by a respirator and he would be nourished from a feeding tube.

We were faced with the question of whether or not Daddy would want to live that way. That question, however painful for us as his wife and children, was easy to answer: he would never, ever want to be left in that condition.

All my experience with doctors, being sick and limited medical knowledge melted away like the false pretense of armor formed from snow. Completely disarmed and vulnerable, I stood there feeling as though I too were melting away in slow droplets. The cornerstone of my foundation, the infrastructure and fortress of my entire family lay upon that bed, kept alive only by the forces exerted upon him by machinery. Just then, OB asked the most poignant, relevant question I'd ever heard: "Doctor, if it were your father in that room, what would you do?"

The doctor was sure that there was no substantial chance of recovery. He added that if it were his father, he might choose to wait until Sunday to make a final decision, though, he stated, waiting until Sunday would only delay the inevitable.

We chose to let Daddy go.

A nurse came to the room and explained the entire process. His body would try to breath of its own volition, she said, and it could last for as long as several hours. Immediately I asked if he would be in any pain. She assured us all that, based on his low percentage of brain function, she was certain he would suffer no pain. The sound I most feared and dreaded was that of his monitors having a "flat line." I asked the nurse to turn the machines off, but for legal reasons, they had to remain on, but would be kept at a low volume.

Family and close friends began to gather outside the room as we braced ourselves for the most horrific event we would ever witness. I'm sure Daddy, in retrospect, would have been touched by the number of people who came that day to support him, and us.

Once inside the room, the issue of family politics began to arise—where would Mommy sit? Where would Nana sit? Where would the kids be in relation to Daddy? I stood next to Nana, in a pair of jeans and a white undershirt, the only clean clothes I had. As the nurse reached to turn off the respirator, I prayed with as much fervency and focus as I could that Daddy would snap out of it—start breathing on his own, open his eyes and get up from that God-damn hospital bed. It didn't happen.

It was obvious once the machine had been removed that Daddy had almost no ability to sustain his breathing. His body began to struggle; though he never emitted a sound, opened his eyes, or gave any indication that he was aware of what was taking place. The mood in the room changed at that point and several people began to cry loudly. Others prayed, while some told Daddy it was ok to go—and that we all love him.

I didn't give a damn about the family politics anymore, and crouched down next to Daddy to lay my hand on his head, partially blocking Nana's view. I had promised him that I would be there with him every step of the way, and this was no different. Daddy once said to me that if he had to walk through the fires of hell, I would be the one he would choose as his walking partner. Nothing could keep me from walking with him, especially now. I began to whisper in his ear, "It's ok, Daddy. You did a great job and you're still the toughest guy I know. Do what you need to do and let go. I'm here for you, and I'll do my best to look after the family. I know you won't forget about us, and we could never forget about you. We'll see each other soon—and I hope it's sooner rather than later. Now go ahead, get going. It's ok." Those were the most difficult words I have ever spoken.

Daddy's breathing began to slow, and his struggle lessened. The color began to drain away from his face. His mouth opened, slightly, as did his eyes. His breathing became very shallow...then stopped. The heart monitor emitted a low, doleful, constant hum. Daddy, the Constant, passed from this earth on Saturday, March 13, 2004.

The next few days were chaotic and overwhelming. We had to pick a funeral home, choose a casket, write an obituary and coordinate the coming and going of various family members. Sue was my only concern. She had difficulty finding a flight, but finally came to my parents' house the day following Daddy's passage. I had no time to cry, let out my anger, or just be quiet and feel his loss. I needed to get out of the house.

Sue and I decided to go to a local restaurant and then take a walk. At the park, we ran into Mr. O'Rourke, one of my teachers from high school. He had read my father's obituary earlier that morning and was walking through the park reflecting on his own father who had passed. Sue, Mr. O'Rourke and I shared a special moment that day, reminiscing about our Dads with love and pride. It was a moment I will not forget.

There were two viewings, one from 2:00 p.m. to 4:00 p.m. and the last from 7:00 p.m. to 9:00 p.m. I didn't anticipate many visitors to the early viewing, but I underestimated Daddy's far-reaching influence. It was packed. There were immediate family, extended family, friends, co-workers, friends-of-friends and all others who'd had any type of association with Daddy. My mother stood tall, taking the time to shake hands with and greet every single person who came to pay their respects. I remember speaking to my friend, Cheryl, in the back of the parlor and watching my mother, who must have been exhausted. She never allowed anyone to see her fatigue but maintained perfect and graceful composure. I remember OB running his hand over Daddy's casket as if he was inspecting it to make sure it was good enough for Daddy.

Megan arranged for the family to have dinner at a restaurant near the funeral parlor. We desperately needed to sit and refuel, and it was good that we did—none of us was prepared for what the 7:00 p.m. viewing had in store.

The moment that the doors were opened, a sea of people poured into the funeral home. The masses quickly became out of control, forcing the parlor staff to form people into lines with velvet roping. I had no idea prior to that evening just how many lives Daddy had touched, or how many people cared for us as a family.

I gave my best attempt to stand at the casket with Mommy and help her greet visitors, but it was useless. I simply cannot recall or estimate how many people were in attendance that night, but nearly every one of them stopped to talk to Mommy. I find the fact that she didn't collapse from exhaustion to be a miracle.

Among the visitors that night was a very old woman, 90 years of age, who had occasionally cared for Daddy when he was a child. Another woman approached me, in tears, hugged me and said, "Oh, my God. When I saw you, I thought you were your father, and that they had made a mistake. I'm so sorry." Still another of my father's friends, an army buddy, was a United States General. I also saw that evening a girlfriend of mine from high school, Kelly, and her husband, brother and parents. Speaking to them, however briefly, was a pleasant reprieve from the passing-by of so many faces; their familiarity was comforting, for certainly there were too many individuals in attendance that night for me to have lived long enough to know them all.

Several people chose to speak that night to share with others how Daddy had touched their lives, and how he would be missed. This is what I wrote:

> Many of you knew my dad as a son, brother, husband, friend, co-worker, or maybe just as an acquaintance. There are some of you who perhaps didn't know my dad at all. Well, it is my honor and pleasure to tell you about him.

If there were a book written about my dad, you would read how he was a mischievous kid that had no problem finding trouble, and whippings had no trouble finding him. You would read that although he suffered from asthma as a kid, he could still run like the wind. He was an average-sized kid who liked picking fights with bigger kids. He lost a lot of those fights, but they prepared him for the fight of his life against cancer.

As my dad grew older, you would read about him as a soldier and devout patriot. He always said he loved three things: "My God, my family, and my country." If it weren't for my mom's influence, my dad would have stayed a military man. However, my parents both agreed it would be better for our family if he didn't. Some of my dad's favorite movies were *Patton*, *Braveheart*, and *Saving Private Ryan*.

Several chapters of my dad's book would be devoted to his love and passion for baseball. He loved watching us kids play baseball, and of course, the New York Yankees. If you asked Dad what he had for dinner the night before, he couldn't tell you, but he could tell you the starting lineup for the 1961 World Champion Yankees. You could read about the promises my dad made to God that he would go to church for a week if the Yankees won the World Series and how he ended up going to church everyday to fulfill that promise. You would read that my dad's favorite player was Mickey Mantle but that he had a special place in his heart for gritty players like Roger Maris.

However, the rest of my dad's book would be dedicated to our family. There would be numerous chapters about my Mom, us kids, and of course, the grandkids. You would read how my dad was the core of our family where we found strength, comfort, and wisdom. He shared in all of our triumphs, tribulations, successes and failures. He was the eyes and ears of our family even after he needed glasses and hearing aids. While he worried about all of us, he protected us. He took care of us better than he took care of himself. And according to him that was the way it should be. You would read that at the center of our good and bad times, our laughter and tears, was Dad: strong and sensitive and always the Constant.

Now that his book is almost complete, I would ask my mom if we could each write our own chapter. I would expect to read that my dad was an awesome guy who touched the lives of many people; how he feared nothing, not even dying; and how he had the heart of a lion. I would read about his bravery and fortitude and his desire to never give up. In my chapter, you would read about the love I have for my dad, how special our relationship was to me, and how I would do anything for the man. You would read how I thought it was my job to bring Dad back when he was in the hospital, as I thought I might be the only one who could. I realize today that Daddy hung in there long enough for us to say goodbye to one another, at least for now. You would read how I will miss him deeply as I not only lost a father—I lost my best friend.

My dad will be in my thoughts, my laughter and my tears for many years to come. To him, I say, "I love you, Dad, and I'll see you soon."

Love,
Danny

The funeral the following morning was excruciating. Aunt Marg recruited a priest from her parish, Father Joe, to say the funeral mass. Father Joe's services were better than phenomenal; I couldn't have been more pleased. Aunt Marg delivered an equally beautiful eulogy that caused us to both laugh and cry. Daddy would have wanted us to laugh.

When we arrived at the cemetery, we were greeted by the sound of bag pipes playing traditional funeral music. It was a sunny day—warmer than it should have been for the month of March. As the piper played "Amazing Grace," we brought Daddy to his burial plot. One of Bridget's close friends, and also a close friend of the family, Mike Bearmore, broke a flower off from the arrangement and gently tossed it down to the casket. I remained standing there, alone with Daddy and the two grave diggers. I looked down upon his beautiful wooden casket, now covered in flowers, and whispered, "Sleep well. I'll see you soon."

I walked directly to the limo and sat inside, hiding in the solitude of its dark tinted windows. I saw through the window my former roommate Jay's wife, Rose, looking for me to say goodbye but unable to find me. I needed to be alone at that moment so I stayed in the car.

After the burial, we did what Daddy would have wanted us to do: we had a bunch of people over, ate a lot of food, and drank a lot of alcohol. We played games and had a karaoke contest. At the end of the night, Sue and I walked upstairs to bed. I fondly remember laying my head on the pillow and smelling what I like to call the "Susie Smell," holding her hand, and falling asleep.

Daddy meant everything to me; so much that I would have given my life to save his in an instant. He was my father; my best friend; my confidant; my competitor; my provider; my care giver; my hero; my inspiration; my Constant. I still catch myself thinking, "I have to call Daddy and tell him what happened." in moments of not wanting to fully realize that he is no longer with us. I often tell stories of Daddy to keep his memory alive and on every March 13th, I say a prayer for him, call him a jackass, and warn him that I am one year closer to coming up there to kick his ass for leaving us. I always close that prayer with, "I love you, Dad and I'll see you soon."

Chapter 13:
Different

AFTER THE FUNERAL, SUE returned to Ireland. Saying goodbye to her was so difficult. I vacillated between extremes of sadness and anger for days. Losing Daddy, the cornerstone of my world, only compounded the pain of watching Sue leave once more.

I soon left as well to complete the final six weeks of my graduate program. It was a Saturday night, black as pitch with rain pounding the car. I missed my turn due to the almost total lack of visibility, pulled over, and in so doing jammed the car in the mud. Three hours later, I made it back to campus, with mud covering the outside of the car, my clothes, and the car's interior. "If this is your idea of a joke, it's not funny." I said to Daddy as I looked up into the stormy night. I felt as though I could hear him laughing, however good-naturedly, at my misfortune.

Over the course of the next six weeks, I was a different person. I was quiet. I made my way to class, back from class, to work and back from work. That was it. When I wasn't doing either of those things, I was drinking. No beer for me: gin, vodka, or Crown Royal martinis. I was so angry—angry that Daddy died and I couldn't bring him back; angry that he would miss my graduation; and angry that he wouldn't even be there to see me have my inevitable transplant. I was also angry that I couldn't have Sue physically by my side to see me through all this. Though drinking numbed the pain and anger for a while, it never killed it; it never killed the pain of losing Daddy, and it never eased my longing for Sue. And with every sip I took, I felt my liver being destroyed. I drank with the goal of destroying my liver, not so I would have a transplant, but so I would die and join Daddy.

Frustrated with it all, I took my relationship with Sue to the brink of extinction. I wanted her to come home more than anything. However, she showed a lack of urgency and effort to make that happen. As we spoke on the phone one particular evening, I was badly depressed. Sue asked what I needed her to do. "I need you to come home," I said. "I can't do this alone anymore." My words had no effect. Sue had a plan as to how and when she would come home, and it was to be no time soon. We began to talk less, and fight more.

On graduation day, an unexpectedly large contingent of my family attended the ceremony. I can only surmise that, knowing how special Daddy was to me, they all decided to support me as best they could. In retrospect I am touched by and grateful for the love my family showed to me that day, though at the time I only felt numb. I explained later to OB that as nice as it was for everyone to attend, I wanted to feel as though Daddy was there also. His absence had torn through my soul, leaving in its wake a bottomless chasm that could not be filled by any amount of alcohol or denial. I questioned whether I was capable of feeling anything at all, or ever would. The realization that Daddy was gone crashed into me like a wall of cinderblocks, and I responded by shoving it further down inside myself.

I wasn't the only one who felt this way; we all took Daddy's passing hard and we all shared the same thoughts— why didn't he stop smoking after we had asked him what seemed like a million times? Why didn't he get an oxygen tank instead of that useless nebulizer? Finally, why was it so hard for him to breathe at times, enough to take his life?

Megan, as much at a loss for answers as the rest of us, at least took the initiative to find them. She reached out to the "Crossing Over with John Edwards" show and secured tickets. John Edwards is a traveling medium who became famous for his skill in supposedly establishing a connection with the deceased and his ability to pass messages from them to the living. Megan attended the show with Mommy and Bridget. As she relayed to me what had taken place during the show, her voice cracked as she explained that Daddy was one of the last to "come through" with a message. In summary, John Edwards shared that Daddy died because he was unable to breathe (he was right), Daddy said that although they (police and medical personnel) were able to "revive" him, it was too late and he was already gone (which I was glad to hear, since it confirmed Daddy wasn't in pain when we removed him from life support). Lastly, John Edwards asked several times, "Who is in business or who works in business?" Megan, Mommy, and Bridget tried to explain that Daddy was a banker but John Edwards said that that wasn't what Daddy was trying to say. After a moment of silence and intense concentration, John Edwards asked, "Who's Dan or Danny?" Mommy explained who I was and that I had just finished getting my MBA. John Edwards responded by saying, "Yes, that's who he's referring to. He would just like to acknowledge Danny, if you would pass that message on to him."

My eyes immediately began to well with tears on the phone with Megan. I was extremely skeptical of John Edwards before they attended the show but I sure as hell wanted to believe in him after that. I have no logical explanation for how John Edwards was able to discern so much information, but he was undeniably accurate. For others who are as skeptical as I was, I want to state as a public record that I have never met John Edwards nor spoken to anyone from his show. To the best of my knowledge, there is no conceivable way his staff could have obtained such a detailed degree of information about my family. I leave it to you to decide whether or not he has a legitimate gift. With that said, I find it hard to bet against him.

Excited to have "heard" from Daddy, it gave me reassurance that he was with me. From that point forward, whether I "felt" Daddy was around or not didn't matter. I did, however, begin to feel more confident that he was indeed somewhere, and was aware of us, aware of me. It was comforting just to feel that he had not forgotten us, just as we would never forget him. I began speaking to him when no one was around and slowly but surely began to feel a renewed, but different, connection with Daddy that I hadn't felt since before his passing. It wasn't as though I had stopped missing him; if anything I likely missed him more. Missing him, as difficult as it was then and still is, at the very least enabled me to begin dealing with the stages of the grieving process, rather than stuffing those emotions away.

The truly positive outcome of the meeting with John Edwards is not whether or not he was able to communicate with Daddy, which is a matter of speculation that can be neither proven nor disproven, but the psychological change that took place within me when I began to feel that there was no longer a gap between Daddy and myself, but a bridge. The "new" relationship with Daddy was understandably not ideal, but it was still something—it was real, but different. Sometimes, different isn't so bad.

Chapter 14:
Time Will Tell

AFTER GRADUATION, I HAD to find a job. The economy wasn't great in 2004 and I knew I would struggle. Sue kindly proposed that I work with her in Ireland for six months while she transitioned home, though there was no definite plan for her to come home in that timeframe. The possibility of being near Sue on a daily basis, although tremendously exciting, soon gave way to practicality. My liver enzymes had increased recently, and the harsh reality was that if I were to become ill while overseas, it would be difficult for me to return to UPenn quickly. The more we discussed it, the more apparent it became that Ireland was too risky from a health standpoint.

The increase in liver enzymes meant a trip to see Dr. Ginsberg. The consummate professional, Dr. Ginsberg greeted me with a handshake and a smile. We exchanged small-talk before digging our heels into the details. I explained that I had been more lethargic lately, with strange pain in my back and side. He asked me to pinpoint for him exactly where the pain was as I indicated that it was directly below my rib cage and on the right side of my back below my shoulder blade. This is where the liver rests, but in an attempt to be optimistic, I suggested the pain might be nothing more than a part of the aging process. Dr. Ginsberg thought differently, and felt the best approach was to conduct another ERCP.

Within two weeks, I was back at HUP, this time with Aunt Marg, filling out the same pre-procedure paperwork that I had scribbled on a half-dozen times or more. A standard questionnaire, it requested information on "... respiratory, cardiovascular, and neurological" problems. The forms consistently irritated me—"Recent cold, bronchitis: NO; pneumonia: NO; history of asthma or wheezing: NO; tuberculosis or silicosis: NO. Who the hell knows what silicosis is anyway? Then again, who knows what Primary Schlerosing Cholangitis is, unless you have it?

The only change in my paperwork was the "Family History" section, where a thin black line very casually demanded to know if my parents were living or deceased. I had all but forgotten about it, until it stared me coldly in the face, a lifeless piece of paper with no sympathy for what my family had persevered through leading up to and following Daddy's death. I held the plastic pen in my hand, hovering over the black line, hating it, and unsure of how to respond regarding Daddy's exact cause of death. He had cancer, but the issues with asthma resurfaced following his lung removal. Aunt Marg felt I should respond with the cause of death as asthma. I did, and filled the empty space of the black-lined paper while probing the wounds of my own still-aching emotional void in the shape of Daddy.

Just then, I was called to the prepping area. I kissed Aunt Marg and rose from my chair, focused on suppressing memories of Daddy. As I lay flat on my back on a surgical gurney, once again giving a concerted effort to seeking pleasantries in the ceiling tiles, I saw Daddy throwing the ball outside with me as a kid. I saw him as a coach when we moved to Bayville and laughing at the jokes we shared. I saw myself saying goodbye to him before his surgery...and crying after his passing. I swore that if a passer-by were to press their ear to my heart, they would be able to audibly hear the torment within me.

The longer I lay there waiting, the less I cared what happened. I knew my liver enzymes were further deteriorating and that the doctors were concerned. I didn't care. Maybe all the drinking I'd done over the last six weeks of school pushed my liver in this direction, I thought. Maybe if I continue to drink heavily I can do myself in and get this over with. As I busied myself considering all my self-destructive options, a nurse came over and interrupted my line of thought by telling me it was time to start the procedure.

Dr. Ginsberg arrived and gave me a rundown of the procedure. I signed the release forms, then was unconscious. When I awoke in recovery, I immediately felt the familiar, searing pain of a Samurai sword in my stomach and knew that I, again, had pancreatitis. "Damn it!" I thought. "Here we go again."

Dr. Ginsberg ordered blood work and confirmed that I did indeed have pancreatitis. I was automatically admitted and waited for a room assignment. Often, I was admitted to a single room due to the complicated nature of my condition. Not so this time, as I saw in the bed adjacent to mine a man who appeared to be far younger than myself. This was extremely disheartening, since all I wanted was some time in solitude. A nurse came in to discuss the protocol for treating pancreatitis: no solids, only intravenal sustenance with narcotic pain relievers administration when needed. Awesome.

My level of frustration grew steadily in conjunction with my level of pain and discomfort. Here I was again staring at another mindlessly boring hospital drop-tile ceiling, in an uncomfortable hospital bed surrounded by beeps, telephones and the maddening click of computer keyboards—and let's not forget, I also had a roommate. However, I would discover that night that my unwanted roommate was more extraordinary that I could ever have imagined.

Aunt Marg came to visit for a while, but she was my only visitor that day. No one expected me to be hospitalized this time. I didn't expect it either—what were the odds, I thought, of having pancreatitis twice? I bet they can't be very good. Next time I should try the lottery—at least then there's a prize involved that whips the proverbial pants off an ass-flashing hospital gown. The only person I truly wanted to see that day, and couldn't, was Daddy.

I quickly discovered that this episode of pancreatitis was different than the first; I found myself hiccupping any time my torso was vertical. If I sat up, I would hiccup. If I walked to the bathroom, I would hiccup the whole way there and back. They seemed to originate from deep within my abdomen, though they were not painful. It did, however, require me to remain fully horizontal until it was absolutely necessary to move.

Pain killers mixed with boredom can cure even the most severe case of insomnia. While hovering between levels of awareness, I awoke to the horrid sound of my roommate moaning loudly and calling continuously for a nurse. My inner voice screamed, "Are you KIDDING ME?!?!? Can someone help this guy or shut him up!!" The nurse came in to talk to him, lecturing him all the while about getting stronger, putting up a good fight and becoming more independent. I took a good look at him, realized how young he was, and wondered why he was there.

Without warning in the middle of the night, I awoke in a tremendous amount of pain and paged the nurse. She administered a shot of Demerol and as we chatted I seized my opportunity to learn a bit more about my roommate. "Hey, is he ok?" I asked, casually. "Yeah, he's ok." she said, "He comes in all the time. He just needs to manage things a little better." I first assumed he was a hypochondriac but thought it rather odd that he looked so young and relayed to the nurse my concern about his age. "Well," the nurse said, "He's only 19 and is on his third liver transplant. He's... doing ok. But I think he may need some help dealing with his issues at times." "You're kidding!!" I said in disbelief. "That's outrageously unfair that someone his age has been through so much." "Yeah," she said, and turned to leave the room, "he's definitely had his share."

What an asshole I was for thinking him a hypochondriac. The longer I lay there looking at the boy's back while he slept, the more infuriated I became with myself for my insensitivity. What is perhaps more tragic than what he suffered from physically was his lack of emotional support to deal with the repeated traumas of surgery and recovery. I thought about Daddy—how he struggled during the last year of his life with physical and emotional challenges. As much as I longed to be the support he needed, I simply could not relate to or identify completely with the unique set of circumstances that my father faced, thereby disqualifying me from being a fully functional support person. At that moment I decided the "poor-me" crap was over and done. I prayed for my roommate to receive the proper support he needed and settled in my mind that no one should ever walk the difficult path of chronic physical illness alone.

After nearly three days in the hospital, the results from my ERCP were available and it became all-too apparent that my liver was in bad shape. The main passageway (common bile duct) had a tight "stricture" that made it difficult for bile to pass through my liver and be processed (referred to as cholestasis). The bile, in turn, was backing up into my internal system and poisoning the rest of my body. This is the normal path of PSC—it closes the liver's passages until it no longer functions. I knew the status of things was deteriorating when Dr. Ginsberg insisted that I make an appointment with the Penn Transplant Center for a pre-transplant evaluation. Despite my best efforts to infer from Dr. Ginsberg's suggestion just how close I was to requiring a transplant, he recommended that I speak to the pre-transplant team. Although disappointed, I respected the fact that his job was to monitor my liver, not take on the job of the transplant team in addition to his own.

As I stepped out of the hospital that day, I did so a different man. My perception of my now deteriorating condition had changed from passive to determined thanks to my young roommate. I chose to no longer feel sorry for myself, nor wallow in self-pity, nor allow Daddy's passing to bring my life to a screaming halt. That day I took the positive step toward facing my illness head-on. On the day of discharge, my baseline enzyme levels were as follows:

ENZYME	NORMAL RANGE	06/24/2004
Total Bili	0.0 – 1.2	3.5
Alk Phos	35 – 125	712
AST	17 – 59	129
ALT	21 – 72	181

Having no idea how to ascertain any grounded information from these numbers, I scheduled an appointment with the pre-transplant team to get some answers.

I called Sue that evening and she immediately vowed to fly home from Ireland to be with me on the day of the transplant evaluation. I vehemently protested, in the understanding that purchasing an international plane ticket on short notice would cost a fortune. Already feeling dejected from my lack of success in finding a job and the fact that my student insurance would soon expire, the last thing I wanted was for Sue to spend an inordinate amount of money to sit with me in the doctor's office. In typical fashion, I lost the argument.

Sue and I arrived at the hospital at 7:00 a.m. sharp on August 2, 2004 and began filling out the tome of necessary paperwork. There would be no plans outside the hospital that day as we moved from station to station, meeting with various members of the transplant team who would administer a myriad of tests.

The first pre-transplant consultation station Sue and I visited was located in a small conference room on the ground floor of the Rhoades building in HUP. As I gazed around the room, trying to guess which members of the eight-or-so families were the patients, I quickly noticed that they all, like me, looked to be in relative good health.

The consultation itself was conducted by a pre-transplant nurse who opened the meeting by handing out a package to each family. The packages contained information about the transplant process, HUP, the HUP team, where to find support prior to and following a transplant, what to expect during the transplant process and what to expect prior to and after surgery. Sue began reading the material as the nurse was still speaking. I peeked over at her, feeling extremely grateful to have an extra set of eyes and ears when my anxiety level was riding high. I knew I could trust Sue to absorb the details, even as I struggled to remain focused.

The second station was the lab, where a urine sample and blood work were required. Thinking nothing of either test, since by this point in my life I had been stuck with more needles than a pin cushion, I filled the cup and sealed it tightly before handing it to the nurse. To my horror and dismay, what was contained in the cup looked nothing like urine—it looked as though I had emptied a can of Coca-Cola. Stunned and petrified to hand the sample to the nurse, I have no recollection of how long I stood in the bathroom feeling certain that with one look, the nurse would immediately admit me to the hospital. I held the cup for Sue to see and she mouthed, in shock, "What's that?!" I mouthed back to her across the room, "My urine sample." Her eyes opened wide with alarm as she sat silently staring at the cup. She then, slowly and with great concern, scanned my body up and down as if trying to see through me into whatever could be so wrong as to cause my urine to turn a sickening tone of blackish-brown.

Reluctantly, I gently returned the cup to the nurse, who was collecting and labeling the urine samples. My sample didn't register with the nurse as unusual at all, and was casually placed aside with the others. I was surprised, but thankful. Though it was highly troubling to me, the reality of the situation was that the nurse had seen hundreds of urine samples just like mine, all coming from imminent transplant patients.

Sue and I were assigned to a transplant social worker, named Laura, who interviewed us both separately and together. We were asked questions such as how long we'd been together, what our long-term plans were and if we were happy. I was also asked, privately, if I had any thoughts focused on harming myself or others. At one point after my father's passing, I had little if any care for my own well-being; but since encountering the young man already on his third transplant, any inclination of harming myself, or others, was completely banished. I was in this for better or worse. I did speak about Daddy to Laura and expressed my pain at his absence. I also spoke of Sue—and how wonderful she was—beyond wonderful. The world seemed slightly more in balance after our conversation with Laura, easing the anxiety of shifting to various exam stations and dispelling any unpleasant preconceived notions of how the day might unfold.

After speaking with Laura, Sue and I spoke to Dr. Burke, a pre-transplant physician who had been assigned my case. Hailing from Ireland, Dr. Burke was witty with a sharp sense of humor; she made Sue and I immediately feel comfortable with both her personality and her vast knowledge of the topic at hand. I, once more, was extremely impressed by the skill and personal level of care the doctors at HUP bring to the table.

The tone of the day changed dramatically when a hospital financial specialist met with us. I tried my best to keep an open mind, having little concept of how high the total cost of transplantation and maintenance could be. This individual, as it became abundantly apparent during the conversation, was in charge of ensuring that potential patients were able to meet the rigorous monetary demands of the surgery in addition to a lifetime of anti-rejection medication. As astonished as I was at the costs involved in such acute care, I was equally as taken aback by the highly impersonal and distant tone of the meeting. It appeared, from the implications of the discussion, that I would not receive the transplant without abundantly sufficient means to pay for it. If I required a transplant to live, but hadn't the means to pay, would the hospital stand idly by and watch me die? I asked no questions and said little. I was more than aware that my student insurance would expire at the end of that month. There was no need to reiterate my already glaring lack of a full-time job with health benefits, or that it could, essentially, kill me.

I later read in my medical records just how the hospital regarded my situation and it was of no comfort:

> "High Concern: patient is a student at PSU, carries Mega Life Ins. under a student plan. Each illness or injury carries a lifetime maximum benefit of $50,000. PATIENT WILL NEED ADDITIONAL COVERAGE FOR LIVER TXP, MAY NEED TO APPLY FOR PA MA. WILL CALL & DISCUSS WITH PATIENT."

"PA MA" stands for Pennsylvania Medical Assistance, also known as Medicaid. Feeling rather downtrodden, Sue and I traveled on to the next station assignment.

Dr. Frank, a resident at the time, would become an attending transplant surgeon in 2005. After examining me, Dr. Frank opened the discussion of a living donor. Potentially, someone from my family could donate a portion of his or her liver which would then be transplanted to me, and in approximately six weeks, both livers would regenerate and grow to normal size. The concept was mind-blowing as I gazed at Dr. Frank incredulously. Immediately, I was overwhelmed with concern and distrusted the notion on the basis that it could place one of my family members in a possibly life-threatening scenario. I nodded and said "Ok." to Dr. Frank, just so we could move to the next phase of the meeting.

Exhaustion began to creep up and solidify its grasp on me as an attending physician was paged for the next conversation in line. It was now mid-afternoon and neither Sue nor I had eaten. I pleaded with Sue to go and at least have a snack at the cafeteria while I waited for the next meeting to begin. Shortly after she left, Dr. Shaked, the lead surgeon of all transplants at HUP, walked in. I was immediately intimidated by both his intelligence and level of skill. Dr. Frank introduced us, and as he shook my hand, Dr. Shaked said, "You look really good. I would bet that you were years away from a transplant. But how do you feel?" "Pretty good right now." I said, "I don't think there's any immediate need for a transplant." He nodded. "Good." he said. "We want you to hold onto your liver for as long as possible. With as good as you look and the nature of your PSC, you could be a year or two away from a transplant, maybe more."

Dr. Shaked then proceeded to raise the topic of living donors. I said I was against it. He pushed back a little, in a professional tone, and explained that overall, the procedure was safe, and should be considered as an option. I asked Dr. Shaked if any living donor had ever died as a result of the transplant. He was honest, and replied that yes, a small percentage of people do die. That was enough for me: the case was closed. I simply would not allow it knowing that there was any risk, however small, of injury or death. However, though the topic was closed in my mind, it wasn't over. It circulated throughout my family and the pre-transplant team for some time before coming to rest.

Dr. Shaked and Dr. Frank left the room shortly thereafter, following a handshake and a formal but friendly goodbye. In the few isolated moments of silence in the room, I felt as though a tornado had touched down and left as quickly as it came. Whether it was due to my being intimidated by Dr. Shaked or the possibility that I would not require a transplant for a few years, I am not sure. Why don't these doctors know for sure when I will actually need a transplant? I asked myself. What if they're wrong? What if I need a transplant now and am being placed on the back burner because of my financial situation? Will I end up dying because of it? Predictably, I began to shut down.

I was at my breaking point. I'd had enough of everything and everyone and was ready to walk out the door, just as Sue walked in through the door. Her presence, as always, was a source of great comfort to me and she convinced me to stay the course, knowing, despite my emotional upset, that it was best.

The gold standard metric for measuring the urgency of a potential transplant patient to undergo surgery is called a MELD score (MELD is an acronym for Model for End-stage Liver Disease). The score ranges from 6 to 40, with 40 being an emergency. It also dictated how high a patient was moved on the transplant waiting list. I did not receive a MELD score that day, though I was administered several other tests measuring the condition of my heart and other major organs and their potential ability to withstand the stress of surgery. In conjunction with my enzyme levels, the MELD score would be heavily used in my future medical monitoring.

Sue and I left the hospital that day physically and mentally exhausted. If anything, the plus-side of spending all day in the hospital receiving tests is that I made significant progress on my "tick sheet," the list of tests I was required to have prior to even being seriously considered for transplant. My concern, however, was that by the time I might be ill enough to require the transplant, all the tests would be obsolete.

It was mentally tiring each time I had to repeat the events of the day to various family members. Everyone was so eager to know how things went, and they so genuinely cared that I couldn't be selfish and deny them the information—but I was dead on my feet by the evening. Perhaps the most troubling aspect of attempting to explain the situation to family was that there was so much unknown—when would I need a transplant? How would I pay for it? Might I NEED to have a living donor? My family did their best to support me, but at times despite their love, and even the love of Sue, I struggled not to feel alone in the knowledge that not one of them truly understood how I felt. Those moments came and passed into the continuous flow of time, and I carried on with my search for a job with benefits while trying to stay healthy in the meantime.

The blood results arrived from the pre-transplant evaluation and I decided to personally monitor them in order to increase my own understanding of how my disease was progressing and how the state of things might stand over the next several months. The ERCP results taken in June, 2004 and the blood work drawn that August showed a sharp differentiation in that my liver enzymes had substantially increased. Here are the results:

ENZYME	NORMAL RANGE	06/24/2004	08/02/2004
Total Bili	0.0 – 1.2	3.5	9.3
Alk Phos	35 – 125	712	938
AST	17 – 59	129	203
ALT	21 – 72	181	173

Months later, I read the write-up from the day of the pre-transplant exam. Below is an excerpt from the doctor's assessment:

> Mr. Bonner is a 31 year-old WM with history of UC and PSC, who has had a rapid decompensation in his liver associated enzymes (LAEs) and has developed jaundice and pruitis. His MELD will likely be greater than 10, which would make him a good candidate for listing for liver transplantation. My concern is that we don't have a clear source of his current decomposition. PSC is a very variable disease and LAEs can vary greatly during the course of the disease. He does not have classic symptoms of Cholangitis, as he reports no fevers, chills, or night sweats. Despite these findings, it is possible that his numbers and symptoms will improve over the next few months.

I was relieved, based on the doctor's description, to know that even if my MELD was greater than 10, at least it wasn't a 35. I don't remember hearing a concrete explanation for the variability of my disease as described, but there it was. Nothing seemed clear anymore. It appeared that the doctors were not even sure if I should be listed for transplant, based on the prospect that my enzyme levels could potentially improve. Only time would tell.

Chapter 15:
That Didn't Take Long

WHILE IN THE HOSPITAL, I received a call to interview with a company I had never heard of for a managerial position in New York City. Sue's brother, Kevin, was in graduate school at NYU at the time, which enabled me to spend time with her on her last day in the U.S. while simultaneously pursuing a much-needed job prospect.

The position, as it turned out, was with a major financial services company. The smaller, unknown company simply recruited employees for it. Frankly, I didn't give a fig about the technicalities of who specifically was offering the job, I just needed work that provided full health benefits.

The interview went extremely well. After walking away I felt sure there was no way in hell I wouldn't get the job. As usual, however, there was a catch: the company hired on a 90-day probationary basis, after which time the new employee would be evaluated, and if determined to have demonstrated a suitable level of skill and desirability, would receive health benefits. The company reserved the right to extend the probationary period, discontinue the contract or extend a full-time offer. Fine. I sucked it up and hoped for the full-time offer.

TGI Friday's was one of my favorite places to grab

greasy but tempting fare, and happened to be located just up the street from where my interview took place at the World Financial Center. I placed an order for chicken fingers and fries, only to quickly realize that I had no appetite.

As Sue and I drove to the airport, my head began to throb with intense pain. The warmth of the sun streaming through the window made me wretchedly nauseous as a shooting pain emanated from my side and back. I hoped desperately my liver wasn't the cause, and decided to drive directly home after tearfully saying goodbye, once more, to Sue.

That night I was scheduled to bartend down the shore but realized it just wasn't going to happen when I began having gripping chills and a high fever. Megan was home and could see I wasn't well. She brought me a blanket and a thermometer that quickly began beeping to register a temp of °103.5. "Should we go to the hospital??" she asked. I chose rather to call Dr. Lokchander's office and have him paged. His opinion was valuable to me and I was ready to do as he suggested. It was after-hours, but within a few minutes the receptionist returned my call to say that Dr. Lokchander was currently doing rounds in the hospital and wanted me there immediately. He also asked the receptionist to tell me that he would not leave for the night until he had seen me. I was immensely grateful and began to gather a few necessities, knowing that I would surely be admitted. Among them was a tooth brush, since the ones provided free of charge at the hospital are too small and feel like steel wool.

Mommy came home as I was in the midst of packing.

She was concerned, as we all were, since the likelihood of my requiring a transplant was at the forefront of our minds and none of us ever knew precisely what the outcome would be during each subsequent hospital visit.

At the emergency room, I registered at the desk then was sent to have my vitals read. When the nurse saw that my temperature was well over °103, she immediately paged Dr. Lokchander and escorted me to a bed. He appeared shortly thereafter and warmly shook my hand, giving me a sense of calm—until the arrival of the infamous peanut butter swirl, which I half-expected. "Do you have blood in your stool?" he asked. Though I quickly responded that no, I did not, he replied, "You probably don't but I have to check anyway." Of course. I had begun to wonder if giving an affirmative answer would prevent having to check for it, since there would be no real reason to doubt me—there can't be that many people in the world who keenly look forward to a thorough finger swooping. Truthfully, I had become numb (almost) to such events by this time and had long since checked my pride at the gastroenterologist's office door.

The next step was liver enzyme testing. Dr. Lokchander explained that a high fever coupled with pain in the side and back could indicate a blockage in the liver ducts. If the blockage was due to the presence of stones in the bile ducts, they would have to be surgically removed. However, if the blockage was due to the beading effects caused by PSC, I would need another ERCP.

Mommy, Megan and OB arrived shortly after Dr. Lokchander left the room and all wanted to know the status of things, but I didn't know anything to tell them. When the blood results were returned, it was confirmed that my liver enzymes were elevated and appeared to be on par with the rates from the pre-transplant evaluation. The only exception was the total bilirubin (TBIL): it had increased from 9.3 to 10.4.

Dr. Lokchander returned later to discuss the blood results with me. He felt certain that I was facing a blockage, and would require another ERCP to open the bile ducts. Soon thereafter I was loaded into an ambulance and sent to HUP.

The nurse at HUP, after administering an IV and helping me settle into my room, assured me that no one would bother me for the rest of the night. On any other night prior to this particular night, those would have been welcomed words. Tonight was different. For the first time, I was filled with a paralyzing fear of being alone. Dark and macabre thoughts swirled through my mind like a howling and malicious wind as I began to imagine what might happen if my liver failed tonight and there was no donor and nothing the doctors could do for me. Daddy was gone. Sue was gone. There was no one to bring me back from the emotional and psychological cliff off of which I felt sure I was about to plunge. Without Sue, I felt tremendously vulnerable to personal catastrophe. Anguished thoughts racked my tortured brain, forcing me to realize that I was completely unprepared for all of this—but could stop none of it. The gravity of the situation barreled toward me all at once, as though I were standing in front of a train with my shoe trapped between the tracks, unable to move out of its deadly path.

Through the night I listened to the hospital's elevator music play softly and hauntingly down the hallways—as monitors beeped, computer keyboards tapped and nurses and doctors were paged over the intercom. I never slept.

I was wheeled to the procedure area shortly after dawn by a very pleasant surgical escort named "Ponch." We struck up a light-hearted conversation that helped to alleviate the anxiety of the impending procedure. I asked him how long he had been working for the hospital, if he had any kids and if so, how old they were. He had been with the hospital for over 20 years, he said, had some kids, but mostly talked about his young son. Ponch insisted he could beat his son at any given game of basketball. "Two out of three," he said proudly. One could plainly see that Ponch was in great physical condition, though I was even more impressed when he confessed to being in his mid-50's. Able to sense my apprehension, he said to me, before leaving me in the appropriate room, "It was really nice talking with you. You look like a strong guy so I'm sure things will be fine. You hang in there, and let me know if you need anything." Touched by his graciousness, I thanked him, and just as quickly, he was gone.

Soon I was greeted by a familiar face on Dr. Ginsberg's team, Dr. Kochman. We spoke briefly about the current situation including the visit with the pre-transplant team and the ERCP in June that once again resulted in pancreatitis.

As Dr. Kochman, the attending nurse and I talked and even cracked a few jokes, I was surprised to discover that, although my insides churned with fear, I found it still easy to connect with people, and began to enjoy my newly found jovial personality in the face of adversity.

A few moments later, I had a mouth guard in place, was positioned for the procedure, administered a sedative, and was unconscious. The main duct traveling into the liver was nearly entirely shut. Dr. Kochman placed a stent to force it open, enabling the fluids to pass through properly. It would need to be removed in six weeks, by way of yet another ERCP.

When I awoke, that familiar samurai-sword-to-the-stomach feeling was unexpectedly absent. I incredulously accepted that I did not have pancreatitis this time around and would be sure to make a note of this to Dr. Ginsberg, who was scheduled to remove the stent in six weeks' time.

Following the stent implantation, there was mixed news concerning my overall condition. The good news: I likely would not need a transplant right away, and certainly wasn't going to die any time soon, notwithstanding an extremely unfortuitous act of nature. The bad news: the clinical diagnosis for my hospital stay was a bout of Cholangitis. My symptoms of unexplainable fever and rigors before being admitted supported this. During the pre-transplant evaluation, it was noted in my chart that I did not display these symptoms, and at the time, that was true.

How my liver would respond once the stent was removed was now the critical question. If it responded positively, there would be no transplant in the immediate future—and if not—well, that would be an entirely different story.

Chapter 16:
My Swan Song

I BEGAN WORK WITH Fidelity (with whom I had recently interviewed) on August 19, 2004. Immediately, I signed up for the health insurance plan that was available to me as a contract employee and felt a huge sense of relief when my student insurance expired on August 31, 2004. I soon relocated to Bayonne with Nana Bonner to be closer to Manhattan; it was comforting, and I loved living there with one exception—Nana was firmly in the habit of eating hot dogs boiled in water, baked beans and French fries at least once a week for dinner. While I appreciated Nana's kindness, the frequency of what was known in our family as "dirty water dogs" was too much to bear.

Six weeks passed quickly, and on the morning the stent was due to be removed OB and I made our way to HUP. Near the hospital were parked several "grease trucks": food vendors for the staff. Unable to eat before a surgical procedure, OB also waited to eat out of respect for me. After waiting for over four hours, the ERCP was finally approved through my newly acquired health insurance. Soon thereafter I was sent to the procedure prepping area.

Dr. Ginsberg soon appeared, reporting that he'd had a conversation with Dr. Kochman, who made sure he related that I did not suffer pancreatitis and that it was because he did the ERCP. We had a laugh about it and after exchanging a few pleasantries, got down to business. I awoke in recovery once more with no signs of pancreatitis. My liver appeared to be responding well, according to Dr. Ginsberg, who later explained to OB and I how the liver fluids continued to flow freely after removal of the stent. In two weeks, I would require blood work to see if that sign of optimism would continue.

During the two-week period following the stent removal, I began to lose weight due to loss of appetite. I was constantly fatigued, and itched over the entire surface of my body. I knew I wasn't doing well, but figured a second stent would be inserted for another six weeks, after which time they would once again evaluate the situation.

Dr. Ginsberg called me at work when the results from the blood tests were available. I had never previously spoken to him over the phone and found his detached presence to be more intimidating than he was in person. He spoke directly, confidently, and without hesitation.

The gist of the conversation was that my liver enzymes had returned to their previously high levels, and re-inserting the stent was no longer a viable option.

The conversation seemed rather surreal as I heard him speak but could not fully process his words and form them into a coherent message. I was in denial; I knew perfectly well what Dr. Ginsberg had to say. My voice began to crack as I tried to talk my way out of reality. Finally, Dr. Ginsberg calmly but quite assertively stated, "I'm sorry, Daniel, but there are no other treatment options for you. You have to contact the transplant center and be listed for transplant as soon as possible." It was strange and oddly disquieting to hear Dr. Ginsberg call me by my full first name. I closed my eyes in an attempt to block those words out of my head and not hear them. It was only October. I had been told in August that I could be years away from a transplant. I certainly wasn't prepared for this.

I managed to mumble, "Thank you, Dr. Ginsberg." and hung up the phone. What transpired over the next three hours was a combination of fear, panic, denial and concession. The fear was first, as thoughts of dying seized me in their cold and unfeeling grasp. Tears filled my eyes as I sat at my desk and thought about all the things I wanted to do that now may never happen: marry Sue, have kids, watch my nieces and nephews grow up...I was overwrought with hopelessness at that moment and needed to speak to Sue. Though I was hesitant to call Ireland from my desk at work, I needed Sue's support more than I was worried about the call showing up on my phone records.

When she answered the phone, I tried to speak calmly in a low tone and managed to smile momentarily when I heard the sweetness of her voice as she said, "Hi, Honey. How are you?" I replied, trying to keep my voice low amidst all the other cubicles, "I'm ok but I could be better." "Talk to me." she said, "Did you hear from Dr. Ginsberg?"

I couldn't find the perfect or most appropriate words to describe my conversation with Dr. Ginsberg so I got to the point quickly. The emotional weight of the phone call increased exponentially as Sue sighed and said, "Oh, Honey.

I'm so sorry," as she began to cry. She did her best to be the rock I needed although it seemed we were a world apart. I went on about my recent weight loss and my complete lack of appetite. For a small, bright but brief moment we laughed as I described my utter disgust for dirty water dogs and swore I would never be able to ingest another one. After reiterating her 24-hour a day availability, Sue and I reaffirmed our love for one another as we hung up the phone. Fear continued to wage war against me as thoughts of death and dying lurked about, essentially incapacitating my ability to do any further work that afternoon.

I sat at my desk thinking about how much I needed Daddy…how much I needed Sue. Under the crushing weight of knowing that neither Sue nor Daddy could be there with me now, at this time when I most needed them, I fell into a tremendous and violent physical display of unabated panic. That cold and unfeeling desk could hardly contain me, though I felt trapped by it, and beneath the sickening glare of industrial fluorescent lighting, I knew that I was among strangers. All I wanted at that moment was to be loved and told that I mattered. I was utterly alone in a crowded New York office, and emotionally alienated. I began shaking at my desk despite desperate efforts to control my muscles for the sake of appearance.

In an attempt to rise out of my panicked state, I began dialing OB, Bridget and Megan, frantically hoping one of them would answer the phone. Megan answered. Upon telling her what had just occurred, she began to cry immediately. "You have to fight as hard as you can, because we just lost Daddy and we can't lose you, too." she said. Her words slashed me like a knife as the realization settled in my mind that the possibility of death was a fear that surged throughout my family, and was not isolated to any of my personal concerns. That meant Sue must be afraid I might die also, but would never say so. Feeling already condemned, I did my best to place a brave mask over my tears, and assured Megan that I would fight every step of the way and would be fine. For just a moment, I began to believe my own words that perhaps I would be.

My manager, well aware of my status as a probationary employee, sat no more than ten feet from me and heard all that was happening. I began to very seriously doubt that I would be employed past the 90-day period now that it was apparent how sick I was. Choosing to at least attempt the path of optimism, I told myself repeatedly that the firm would recognize my value as an employee and stand by me.

At 5:00 p.m., I quietly packed my things and began the journey home. Denial began to have a grasp on me as I thought over the day's conversations. During the pre-transplant meeting, Dr. Shaked had told me rather confidently that it could be years before I required one. If I just fought hard enough, I thought, I might be able to not only make it through the 90-day probationary period but also repel a transplant for several months or longer. By then, I would have full health benefits. By the time the light rail stopped at 22nd street, I was convinced I could do it and actually had a bounce in my step.

Nana Bonner was on her way out to a function as we

met each other at the door. She could have run for mayor and won with how many people she knew. "Dinner is on the stove!" she said, as I thanked her and kissed her goodbye.

I cautiously approached the kitchen, fearing the worst but not wanting to ruin the optimistic state into which I had willed myself. Immediately, the wretched smell of boiled hot dogs burned in my nose and just as quickly my emotional world fell apart. The reality of my health situation came crashing down as the strength in my legs collapsed, and I crumbled into the nearest chair. My skin was yellow; I was unbearably itchy; and I continued to drastically lose weight without trying. I needed a transplant. It was real. I was real, and this was truly happening to me.

Calling Sue from Nana's line must have cost a small fortune, but the moment required it, and I knew Nana would understand.

Sue picked up the line and I said, "Hi, Honey. You're not going to believe this, but..."

"You have dirty water dogs for dinner." she interjected.

I answered her wearily, "I just can't do it tonight."

"Oh, Honey!" she said with love in her voice. We began to laugh. I laughed at the irony of my misfortune, of hearing that I could potentially die followed by a hearty meal of those god-damned boiling wieners. It *was* funny. We talked for a few more minutes, trying to keep it short for the sake of Nana's phone bill, and formulated a strategy.

I took the dirty water dogs and baked beans and put them in the garbage, then promptly took the garbage bag down to the garbage bin and replaced Nana's garbage bag with a fresh one. Then, after disposing of the evidence, I walked to Burger King, ordered a fried chicken sandwich, sat there and ate it. When I returned home, I was exhausted and fell asleep quickly though it was still mid-evening.

It was early October. My main goal was to make it to the 90-day probation mark and obtain health benefits. In addition to that I had to inform the rest of my family about the change in my status, as well as help Sue plan her trip home. After informing the hospital that I required transplant, the next step would be to remain as healthy as possible to increase my chances of not only making it to transplant, but surviving such an intense surgery.

At some point in the autumn, Megan and the kids moved to North Carolina. Bridget and her family were also planning to move from New Jersey to Tampa, Florida. Jarlath, Bridget's husband, was forced to relocate earlier than she was due to the starting date of his new job. Knowing that she needed help packing, I volunteered, believing the change of pace and scenery would do me some good. What no one knew is that I had carefully planned my day, with every intention of drinking myself into oblivion that night, alone, for the very last time. It would be my swan song.

After helping Bridget, I returned to my mother's house and didn't have to wait long for her to head upstairs to bed. By 10:00 p.m. I began my drinking mission with a Tanqueray martini, then moved to whatever beer was in the back of the fridge and ended the evening with a few Mike's Hard Lemonades.

It didn't take long for the alcohol to effectively intoxicate my dwindling frame; I became irate just as quickly as condemning thoughts of my inability to prevent Daddy's death plagued me. I was typically an angry drunk, and this bout was no different than all the others. One would think that my health would have been the major impetus for such aggression, but it was the overwhelming self-imposed conviction that I had let Daddy down so tremendously that caused me to spiral out of control.

As I stood in the same kitchen where he collapsed, I tried to reenact the night he died, tracing what I was told were his last steps. I struggled under the influence of the alcohol to discover what might have been done differently. If I'd had just one more chance, I would have been able to bring him back. I failed.

The image of his fall to the kitchen floor played mercilessly through my mind, repeating itself in a sinister way that brought my frustration to the precipice of total despair. As these toxic emotions surged through my being, I lost all sense of composure and bounded up the stairs to Mommy's bedroom where I banged my fist against her door until she answered. I cried out that it was my fault Daddy had died, and if I could have done more, perhaps he might have lived.

I could see the heartache on her face as she calmly listened to me: here was her son, drunk, banging like a lunatic on her bedroom door in the middle of the night. I was unable to cope with needing a liver transplant, reeling from the loss of my father and looking for my mother, who had lost her husband and could potentially lose her son, to say the right thing at the right moment as only Daddy could do. Never had I expressed to anyone how I really felt about Daddy's death, especially Mommy.

She took me in her arms, repeating softly how it wasn't my fault and that there was nothing I could have done differently to stop the sequence of events. It was just "Daddy's time" she emphasized to me. My mother's incredible strength and fortitude in the face of such adversity and loss were truly commendable. I just couldn't bring myself to accept what felt like a weak excuse, that it was just "Daddy's time."

I left Mommy's room and returned downstairs to start calling anyone who might answer the phone. OB was working; I then tried to call OB's girlfriend, Jennie, but mistakenly dialed my mother's friend Linda. Finally, I called Sue, knowing that it was just before dawn in Ireland. Sue answered, fulfilling her promise to be always available. She was lovingly angry that I had gotten drunk "in my condition" and had no hesitation to say so. Still in the grip of the alcohol and still feeling angry, I spoke harshly to Sue, saying, "You have no idea what I'm going through because you aren't here! So who are you to tell me how to live my life!" I still regret how, in my drunkenness, I manipulated the situation to make Sue feel guilty for not being physically near me. She, however, maintained her temper as I continued to rant.

Sue's breaking point came when she heard me open the refrigerator door to look for whatever bottles I might have left behind. "Do you really think you need that drink?" she asked. I replied, pissed that she was attempting to bring me to my senses, and said, "I don't need it, but I want it." She hung up, unwilling to take further part in my self-destruction.

The following morning, I avoided the entire situation by bringing donuts and bagels to Bridget's house, ate, and got to work. Bridget was understandably concerned about my dangerous behavior, but never appeared judgmental. Rather, I had the distinct impression that she was sympathetic and on some unspoken level understood why I chose to do what I did.

The frustration and pain I felt the night I chose to drink and so horribly damage my already decaying liver were followed by feelings of unquenchable guilt. I was fully aware that I had let not only Sue, but Daddy and the entire family down and had destroyed their faith in me to fight the good fight and play by the rules. That was the way Sue had wanted it. That was the way my family and certainly Daddy would have wanted it—for me to conduct myself honorably through a time of trial while always hoping for the best.

Though I knew I had disappointed all those dear to me, their love compelled me still to believe in redemption and second chances. From that day forward I made the decision to change for the better, for the sake of their love if not for my own benefit.

Chapter 17:
Thanks for Nothing

IN EARLY NOVEMBER, SUE told me that she had been offered a position with Merrill Lynch in the World Financial Center. I was elated beyond the capacity of mere words that after all the tears, the fights, the long-distance conversations, traveling and coordination, Sue would finally be home. Due to return the week before Christmas, I certainly could never have asked for a more precious gift.

It was during this time that the news of my near-critical condition had traveled its way through both my immediate and extended family. As a result, most of them placed calls into HUP volunteering to be my living donor. Despite the fact that I remained adamant in my refusal to risk the life of a family member in order to obtain a donor, I could not stop them from volunteering. I would later be shocked and humbled by the number of my relatives who selflessly offered a part of themselves, at the risk of their own health to help me.

In order to be considered as my living donor, the minimum requirements were that the person be relatively the same size as me with a compatible blood type. I stand about 5'10" and weighed in at that time at approximately 180-190 pounds with a B+ blood type (only 1 in 13 people are B+, making it relatively uncommon). Sue, Mommy,

OB, Bridget, Megan, Uncle Mike, Aunt Marg, Uncle Tom, Aunt Mary and my cousins Tom, Mike, Chris, and even Nana Bonner's tenant, Charlie, all placed calls into HUP to volunteer as a living donor. If not ruled out by the minimum set of requirements, the next level was rather stringent and more difficult to pass. If, after surpassing the minimum criteria the individual also passed a series of physical and psychological tests, that person would be the living donor candidate.

Immediately, Mommy, Uncle Mike and Aunt Marg were too old. Bridget, Megan and Aunt Mary were too small (at between 5'0" and 5'4" inches, their small bodies could not function with the amount of liver that would have remained after removing enough to support the size of my body). Uncle Tom had too many health problems (high blood pressure and cholesterol). Sue was not seriously considered because of her potential role as my primary caregiver following the surgery. That left OB and my cousins as the top contenders.

OB deeply wanted to be my living donor for several reasons: Daddy, OB and I were all alike. There were slight differences between us, but overall, there were many more similarities. Such a unique connection cannot be easily explained except to say that, as is often said in literature, we were kindred spirits, and intimately connected to one another in a way that transcended the bond of blood. OB and I were not able to prevent Daddy from dying, and that fueled OB's desire to save me at whatever cost. He felt it was his duty and obligation to be my living donor, just as I thought it was my duty and obligation to save Daddy.

I very much valued and was touched by the dedication that OB showed. If it had been possible and safe for me to have a living donor, I would have wanted OB to be that person. I would have wanted him to be proud of what he had done for me and for the experience to have brought us closer. I began to look forward to the jokes in the family that would arise out of my having OB's liver. I pictured newspaper articles written about us, just as when we were kids playing on the same baseball team, and I envisioned myself telling my own kids how he had saved my life.

It was not to be. At 5'8" and approximately 250 pounds taking several medications including those for high blood pressure, OB was quickly disqualified. OB was deeply disappointed and I was disappointed for him. I asked him not to worry himself over it, since I had staunchly refused a living donor and would continue to do so, but he wanted none of it. The pressure he placed on himself after that day only grew stronger.

I had hoped the search for my living donor would end with OB but it did not. My cousins Tom, Mike and Chris were all considered as potential donors and it looked increasingly likely that one of them would be chosen.

Chris was quickly removed from the list due to his active student status at New York University. Tom had run track at Georgetown, specializing in the 800 individual and 4x800 relay races; he was in phenomenal shape and was the correct height, weight and blood type. Mike was a member of the United States Coast Guard, exceptionally conditioned and also filled the height, weight and blood type criteria.

As the living donor investigation continued against my will, I continued to concentrate on my own list of accomplishments. Before I could be listed for transplant, there were several tests I needed to undergo, in addition to determining my ever-tremulous health insurance situation. The hospital had made it clear that I would require a higher level of coverage before transplant. While they did a tremendous job of preparing me physically, the emphasis on the financial aspect of my condition made me feel like a lesser being, readily dismissed if my inability to pay were to become apparent.

Outside of the hospital stuff, I needed to work things out with Sue. There were many questions floating around concerning where she would live, as well as where I would stay following surgery since I would be temporarily unable to care for myself. These questions weren't going to be answered right away but they were definitely in the forefront of my mind.

The pressure to stay physically functional and secure full health benefits at Fidelity was crushing. I began to feel as though I were running a race against my own body, which was deteriorating at an alarming rate. I continued to lose weight and body mass with my skin and eyes yellowing significantly; my urine was extremely dark and my strength had diminished. Often, I was so tired following a day at work that I would fall asleep by 8:00 p.m.

The worst and most unrelenting of my symptoms was the incessant itching. It had spread over the surface of my body encompassing areas I could not easily reach such as my back, and intensified when I would perspire. I once described the itchiness to a friend as feeling like a million mosquitoes in my blood stream, biting me from within. Nothing could alleviate it as I scratched those areas raw to the point of bleeding. Someone in the family eventually bought me a soft-bristled body-brush to use for scratching after witnessing the claw marks that covered my arms and legs.

In an effort to remain reasonably fit, I began exercising as much and as often as I could withstand. I ran, lifted weights or rode my bike—anything to keep moving. As the sweat would bead over my head and arms, especially while running, the itching was unbearable. Normally after a workout, I would return home, shower and sleep, unable to exert any further energy.

Each day was an uphill battle that began the moment my feet touched the floor. I was physically able to walk around, take a shower, dress myself and go to work; I simply had no desire. I was forced to search deep within myself and tap into what small resources of strength and fortitude I had still remaining. The days grew progressively more difficult as my mental and emotional energy began to fade in parallel with my fading body. When the day was over, I would crash on the bed and sleep hard until the morning.

Toward the end of November, my 90-day probationary period at Fidelity was nearly complete. I felt I had done a good job managing my people and adding value to my position. There was no reason not to expect a formal offer.

The week before Thanksgiving, my manager called me into a conference room to discuss my situation. I considered

Gifted

what my starting salary would be, though it paled in importance to the health benefits. "Which health plan should I choose?" I thought, while also thinking of the best time to take a few vacation days near Christmas to be with Sue and the rest of my family.

When we sat down, I had a pen and paper ready to take notes if necessary. The manager began the meeting by saying, "I wanted to meet with you about your contract..." I could hear in her voice that something was clearly amiss and my heart pounded with sickening anticipation. Her hands began to shake and she no longer looked me in the eyes. Rather, she stared at her papers as though she was reading from a script.

Though my heart initially raced with fear, it quickly turned to unspoken rage when I surmised the direction that this meeting would take. If the decision was made to fire me, I wanted to hear her say the words while looking me dead in the eye. "Look at me and say it, you coward," I repeated silently to myself as though trying to will her to stop staring at the blank pad before her and speak as a human being with real words, not using the mouth piece of corporate bullshit she had been told to use as the firm's security blanket.

After stumbling over her words for nearly a minute, she finally said, "We've decided not to renew your contract." An extremely awkward silence followed—I know she was prepared for me to explode in anger (God knows I wanted to), yet all I said was, "Ok." I had hoped, as a result of my unexpected behavior that she might just say I was not being renewed because of my health condition. I pleaded in the midst of that terrible silence for her to say I was being let go for not having satisfactory job performance—if she would even slightly mix her words in some inappropriate way, I thought, I could march directly to Human Resources. Had she even hinted at the reality of the situation that is precisely what I would have done, but she did not. Her statement was politically correct and well planned in advance by either Legal or Human Resources. She said, with her eyes darting around the room, "The firm is looking to make some personnel changes, and your position is being restructured." Her statement ensured that the firm was now protected should a potential lawsuit arise.

Stewing with anger, I asked, "Ok, when is my last day?"

"Monday after Thanksgiving." she replied.

I chuckled at the ridiculousness of this statement. I was thinking, "Thanks for nothing," but said, "I will not be returning after Thanksgiving."

She sighed with an air of relief and said, "Ok, that's fine."

I tried to remain the consummate professional, though the rage I felt could have melted her face had it been unleashed.

During our "conversation," the manager kept looking at a folder of paper as if trying to find the right words to say. When she finally looked up, I wanted her to look deep into my yellow eyes. I wanted her to see the fire behind them. I wanted her to see my physical pain. I wanted her to see how hard I had worked just to stay healthy enough to make it to this stupid meeting. I wanted her to see my disappointment. Most of all, I wanted her to see me for what I am - a human being. That job literally meant the world to me: it was a lifeline that was now gone. I wanted her to see it all.

As the meeting ended, she appeared to be more relaxed. After all, I had neither exploded nor fought back. When our eyes met I stared at her, with a look not of rage or malcontent, but one of openness. I believe, as she looked into them, that she saw the message I desperately tried to relay without speaking a word. "Remember this look," I thought as I held her in my gaze, "and ask yourself how you could, in good conscience, let me go."

Did she feel guilty for terminating me? Did she feel badly because of how I looked and in turn, how I must physically feel? Perhaps she felt neither, or both. Whatever she felt, I believe my eyes convincingly told the story of one who had worked as hard as anyone could to make it to the finish line and the death sentence she had now imposed upon me.

That evening I made my way home with a sense of urgency, not wanting the manager to see me shed even one tear. I called Sue, and began to cry before she was given the chance to answer. After drawing a few deep breaths, I managed to tell her the story. She was struck with horror but collected herself rather quickly, reminding me all the while that she would be home soon to walk this journey beside me. I could not hear her. Nothing she said was able to afford me any comfort, for I felt as though I was already dead.

Nana had prepared dinner but I was unable to compose myself sufficiently to sit at the table and chat. I kissed her, explaining that I was tired from the strain of the day and went off to bed.

I lay that night in bed gazing at the ceiling seeking patterns in the tiles as was my habit in the hospital. How I would survive, or if I would survive this ordeal was unclear. The longer I lay still on my back in the darkness, the more terrifyingly real it seemed to me that my fate was not to be married or have children, because in an undisclosed but relatively short amount of time, I would die. I wanted to live—more than anything I wanted to live—and as we live and journey along the individual paths of our lives, we discover that so frequently the human invention of language cannot adequately express the depth, fervency or boundless nature of raw and tender emotion. I was at odds with myself that sad night as I struggled in the abyss of my emotional prison to rectify beyond the limitations of language that the circumstances surrounding me were real: I was in very real danger of death. The tremendous weight of groping along the walls of my reasoning in search of an answer in culmination with the tangible blackness of the bedroom proved too immense, and as I was enveloped and blanketed in these dark waters my mind found respite in the silence of sleep.

The following morning, I gave serious and rational thought to Fidelity's decision. From a human perspective, their decision was unethical and falsely biased against me due to circumstances outside of my control. I had been hired to do a job and did it well; I possessed the desired skill-set for

213

the position and added value to the organization. I wasn't a slacker.

From a business perspective, I agreed with their decision. The firm had a job to fill. If I was absent for six or more months, it would cause an undo hardship on the company. Fidelity's business model, I feel certain, does not include taking on sick employees for the purpose of paying their medical expenses. They are a profit-seeking firm looking only to increase shareholder value; they are not a charitable institution with the mission of curing diseases or embarking on feel-good humanitarian projects. Therefore, maintaining my employment would have also imposed a burden on not only my department, but on the shareholders as well.

Ultimately, I felt that Fidelity had made the right decision, purely from a business perspective. When business and the fragility of human life come into conflict with one another, I have chosen to believe that those times are never easy for the firm, and certainly not for the individual who has been chosen to deliver the message.

However, with newly found time on my hands, I decided to spend Thanksgiving in Ireland with Sue. She spent hours preparing a traditional American Thanksgiving dinner which I enjoyed immensely. Sue's friends also came to dinner, and a fine time was had by all. I was given the opportunity to visit with Jarlath's brother Gavan, who is a good friend, and Sue's friends Lorna and Sinead. I left Ireland with a fresh and rejuvenated spirit. Though still in a state of chronic physical exhaustion, my will was renewed and I felt more able to tackle the pressing issues that lay ahead.

Chapter 18:

The Spaghetti Spirit

UPON RETURNING HOME, MY first stop was to visit
HUP and be examined to determine the seriousness of my
current state. I met with several physicians including Dr.
Burke and Dr. Shaked. My main complaint to Dr. Burke was
the horrendous and incessant itching that at times made me
feel as though I might lose my mind. There was medication to
alleviate those symptoms, she assured me, but not wanting
to appear as though I couldn't "handle" it, I refrained from
telling her exactly how severe it was.

When Dr. Burke asked about my employment situation,
I told her the story about my job. She was supportive and
relayed to me that she had planned to place me on medical
disability regardless of what happened with my job. I
wouldn't be capable of working for much longer.

I next met with Dr. Shaked. He was gracious, and
apologized for stating it may be years before I required
transplant. It was surely not his fault. The very nature of
PSC is highly variable; it progresses differently in different
people and symptoms can come and go without warning.
When considered in conjunction with the fact that I
remained physically fit, my episode of rising enzymes in
August could have simply been another fluctuation of PSC's
temperamental behavior; there was no way that Dr. Shaked
could have predicted otherwise.

I found myself deeply moved by our meeting. Dr. Shaked radiated compassion, positive energy and excellence. In fact, I was so taken with Dr. Shaked that I was compelled to know more about his career, and found his medical history and experience to be nothing less than extraordinary.

Dr. Shaked obtained his M.D. in 1982 and received a Ph.D in Molecular and Cellular Pathology/Immunology in 1989. He served as Head of Transplant Surgery at HUP, which was mentioned previously, as well as President of the National Association for Transplant Surgeons. Dr. Shaked is an incredible doctor, and an equally wonderful person.

Eventually, questions arose once more concerning how I planned to pay for the transplant. The feelings of frustration and helplessness made me explosively angry; I wanted to scream: "I'M WORKING ON IT!! NOW GET OFF MY CASE!!"

However, the hospital was attempting to help. Their job now was to assist me in securing an alternative or at least place me on the correct path to helping myself.

Two programs were recommended to me, one in which the requirement was to be a resident of Pennsylvania, and the other the federal Disability Insurance program through the national Social Security system.

The drawback is that disability benefits were not synonymous with health benefits. As opposed to paying a monthly premium and receiving health care, a monthly check would be delivered to me that could in turn be used to pay for medical expenses. One was required to remain on disability for a minimum of six months before collecting any funds. Based on the rate at which I was deteriorating, there was no way I would live another six months in order to receive assistance. I left the hospital that afternoon once more crestfallen and mired in dejection.

As my family began to learn of the situation, my mother began looking into refinancing her house. I investigated the possibility of cashing in my retirement account as a down payment, while others offered to open their checkbooks and help in any way they could. It was a highly stressful, humbling period in my life and one that affected all members of my family. The fact that my mother, as well as other family members, considered steps as drastic as refinancing their homes or reaching into their retirement accounts for the sake of my transplant made me feel that I was simply not worth so much trouble. Fortunately for me, they felt differently. I would later learn that Aunt Mary's sister, Nan, who was a highly successful executive at a major financial firm in New York, offered to pay for the transplant solely at her own expense. Her gesture to finance the surgery cannot be adequately explained in mere words, for it was purely angelic.

Shortly after resettling, Mommy announced that she was planning to sell the house and move to North Carolina to be closer to Megan. My original plan had been to remain with her following surgery to recuperate. Though I had also considered living with Sue, after not having spent significant time together in years, we both felt it would be best to first live in close proximity, though not necessarily together. As was the case with Nana Bonner, I also did not want to burden

217

Sue with my full-time post-operative care. That, in my mind at least, wasn't the best way to keep a fiery romance alive.

One morning as Mommy and I sat at breakfast, I could tell that she was anxious for me to confirm that her decision to sell the house and move was the correct one. I chose my words carefully, never thinking that she would actually follow through with any of it. After reasoning that I had planned to live with Sue, leaving her with no real reason to stay, Mommy then uttered a sentence that left me stunned and silent in disbelief. "I can't just sit around and watch my son die," she said. "Is she serious?" I thought to myself over, and over, and over again. I was devastated and finally settled in my mind that if Mommy wanted to go to North Carolina, she should just go.

If Daddy had still been living during the time of my surgery, I was certain that he would have wanted to be as close to me as was physically possible, down to scrubbing in with the doctors if given the opportunity and moving into my hospital room while I healed. Mommy was different. She seemed to desire more space, both geographically and emotionally, as my condition became ever more severe.

By mid-December, I was still without any palpable leads for health insurance. I had nearly resigned myself to dying, when one day I discovered several plans offered through the State of New Jersey. I decided to apply for one of the PPO plans listed on the website through Oxford Health Plans. The Oxford plan appeared to cover surgery, hospitalization and medication. The premiums were high (between $400 and $500), the co-payments were reasonable, and there was an out-of-pocket maximum of $10,000 for all services. Considering that the cost of undergoing a transplant can easily exceed $250,000, this was a bargain. I filled out the application and submitted it; the only thing left to do now was wait.

One night during the week, OB called and asked if I wanted to go to a basketball game at the local high school that evening. As a fundraiser, the high school teachers were to play against the teachers from the middle school. It presented a good opportunity for me to get out of the house and distract myself from my problems for a while.

After the game I ran into a friend of mine from my school years, Tom. He and I had taken the same classes and played football together. Now he was the Principal of Central Regional Middle School. When he saw me, he shook my hand and asked how I was and if there was anything he could do. He was sincere, and I appreciated his graciousness, though I responded that I was fine. Tom saw through my façade and said kindly, "There's got to be something we can do for you." Once more I thanked Tom for his words of kindness and attempted to ask how his family was doing and how he liked being Principal. "Everything's fine," he said. "We've definitely got to do something for you." He wouldn't take no for an answer as we cordially shook hands and said goodbye.

The following day, OB called to ask what I had planned for Tuesday night. My first reaction was to cringe, since one never knew what OB might have up his sleeve. Reluctantly, I admitted that I had no plans, but since Sue would be home by then, things may well change. "Be at the high school Tuesday. No option." said OB. The truth of the matter is that I did not want to have any plans, in order to leave the night open for Sue. In response to being pushed I became irritated with OB, insisting to know what the hell was so important.

He blurted, "Tom asked for permission from the school board to have a spaghetti dinner to raise money for your surgery. It was approved and it's happening Tuesday night." I had to sit down. After a moment of silence I caught my breath and confirmed the time. I then quickly hung up, overcome by the emotion. My first reaction was one of pride. I felt disappointed in myself that I hadn't been able to "straighten out" my own situation up this point, forcing me to be in need of the kindness of others. I didn't want people to sit around eating spaghetti feeling sorry for me.

I then softened and began to think of how remarkable it was that Tom had managed to approach the school board and organize an event of this scale within five days. It was truly a testament to his character that he meant what he said and was a sincere, genuine individual. I was humbled by, and grateful, for his actions.

Between Nan's tremendous offer to pay for the surgery and Tom's organization of the dinner, I was overwhelmed by the generosity of others. I never liked being the center of attention and felt undeserving, though others clearly felt otherwise. Perhaps the harsh outlook I imposed upon myself wasn't the healthiest attitude of self-worth, but it was nevertheless how I felt.

How joyful I was when Sue returned home. I feel certain that despite the life-threatening severity of my illness and my yellow skin, I glowed when Sue walked through the door, this time to stay. No more tears, no more planes, no more international calls. She was home.

Upon learning that my mother was selling her house and moving to North Carolina, Sue was shocked. She had just returned home and was now told that I had no place to live following surgery. I resented this fact, since I had not wanted Sue to feel forced or coerced into living with me, but wanted her to decide when she felt the time was right. After five years abroad, Sue would now have to begin a new job and locate her own place to live. To thrust upon her the additional responsibility of intimately caring for someone following a major surgery felt unfair to me.

Word of the spaghetti dinner spread quickly. My dear friend, Tooch (Paul), and his wife, Lori, donated four custom-made gingerbread houses for a raffle. My friend Willie, with whom I also played football in high school, planned to DJ the party, while so many others offered to decorate, cook, set-up, clean-up, and assist in any way they could. I was truly touched. One of the school's administrators was related to the then-governor of New Jersey, who heard about my lack of health insurance. He reached out to the executive office and the morning of the dinner I received a call asking for information about my plight. The woman took my number, provided some suggestions, and offered to personally handle my call if I needed additional assistance.

I realized after speaking to a member of the governor's

office that this event had become the embodiment of the holiday spirit: it was warm, giving, compassionate and contagious. Everyone was excited to be involved and it had become a rallying point for those who wanted to help but didn't know how. For the first time in a long while, I felt like a truly special person.

The night of the dinner finally arrived, and though I wanted to appear well-dressed, the clothes hung off of my gaunt frame as I searched for something suitable to wear. I finally settled on a pair of black pants and a pale grey shirt, which did no service to my yellow skin.

As the dinner approached that evening, I became increasingly uncomfortable with the amount of trouble to which I felt others had gone on my behalf. Just as Daddy had been the Constant, I felt I should be the Constant, and I wanted to be. I wanted to be admired for my warrior spirit and ability to weather my circumstances and emerge triumphantly, not to be pitied. Though I wanted to proudly wear the badge of the Constant, I certainly did not feel up to it the night of the dinner. I felt like a sham, and was sure others could see through my façade.

Sue arrived a half-hour prior to the dinner. I studied her every step as she walked up the driveway to the house in a long, fitted denim skirt and a black top. She was beautiful. I swung the door open as she stepped toward me and seized her, taking her in my arms and taking in every second that passed while she was in them, relishing that she was finally home for good. The simple sight of her was healing, and as I felt, kissed, and breathed in the scent of her I was overcome with emotion and wanted to hold her forever.

We talked for a short while and then departed for the dinner. At the school, a young student sat in a folding chair at the entrance collecting a $5.00 fee for admission. Sue, in her graciousness, passed a $20.00 bill to the girl and in we went. It was then, as we passed through the doors, that I was met with what seemed a sea of people in every direction—well over 200. Some were buying and selling raffle tickets, some served dinner, while still others were chatting, eating and mingling near the DJ booth. I took a few breaths to compose myself and hugged Sue, whispering in her ear, "Now what do I do?" She whispered back softly, "You should grab something to eat and start mingling—you have a lot of people to greet." "I'm on it." I said, as we approached the food line. Almost instantaneously I saw Mommy, Nana Pawlowski, OB, Jennie, Jennie's friends Laura and her husband Jeff, along with several of my teachers from high school. Near the salad line I saw Mrs. Fitz, my high school sweetheart's mother. It was touching to see so many with whom I had lost contact over the years and who now gathered to support me.

Though I tried my best to speak with each guest individually, the task quickly became overwhelming and as I looked above the crowd to locate Sue, I saw Tooch and Lori standing with Sue just outside the kitchen. They gestured for me and I excused myself as politely as I could. There stood Paul's mother and sister, along with their two young daughters, Kelsey, five-years-old, and Carly, who was three. Kelsey looked up at me with brownish-blonde hair and large brown eyes. I worried that she was staring at me because she was afraid of my appearance. "Daddy said that you were sick and needed some money to pay for the doctors so you can get better. I got this from my piggy bank and I want you to have it." With that, she pulled from her pocket three $1.00 bills. Tears immediately filled my eyes and I knelt down to hug Kelsey tightly, mainly so she wouldn't see me weeping. "Thank you so much, Kelsey. This helps me a whole lot," I said, "I can't thank you enough." As I stood, I saw that the faces of everyone near me were also dampened with tears. How could they not be? It was the sweetest and most pure gesture of giving that I had ever witnessed.

Tooch then said:

> I told the girls you were sick and needed to see a doctor, but that doctors cost a lot of money. When I told Kelsey there would be a spaghetti dinner for you to raise the money, she asked how much it cost. I said it was five dollars. She went running up the stairs to her piggy bank and came down with three singles. 'This is all I have.' she said, 'Is it enough?' Through my teary eyes I said it was plenty and we made our way here. I never told her what to say—it was entirely from her heart.

As Tooch told the story, tears continued to fall from my eyes. I knew I had to pull it together with so many others waiting to speak to me that night—but it was nearly impossible. I will never forget Kelsey, that moment, and how much it still means to me.

As an infant, Kelsey would not tolerate being away from Lori, and would cry whenever I was around. As she grew older, she became closer to me and when I would visit Tooch and Lori, we would play with her dolls and have a great time. Once, she asked me to bring her to the "little girls' room," which terrified me since I wasn't comfortable around naked kids or, really, nakedness in general. I stood outside and waited my turn. When she was finished and had come out, I went in. "Did you wash your hands?" she asked in the tiny voice of a three-year-old. "Why, yes I did!" I said, and she took my hand as we walked to the other room.

After parting with Paul, Lori and the girls, Sue and I made our way to the main food line. In the serving area stood my high school sweetheart, Kelly, slinging spaghetti and meatballs on the rows of empty plates before her. I introduced her to Sue and we shared a pleasant, though brief, conversation as others waited to receive their servings. It meant a lot to me for her to be there.

As I sat down at the table with a delicious, hot pile of pasta, I felt suddenly ungrateful. Was I adequately verbalizing my immeasurable thanks to everyone who had attended? I wasn't able to even speak to them all individually, much less thank each person separately. The dinner, the time that everyone had so freely dedicated to my cause—it all meant so much. I felt somewhat frustrated, as though the immensity of my feelings were trapped within my limited body, unable to be seen and felt by all who attended that night as fully as would be appropriate in response to such communal generosity.

More people flowed to my table after dinner. Aunt Moe attended after having driven for hours. I saw our family friends Mike Bearmore, Mr. Frulio (in a Mets jacket), Tom and Karen Reidy and their family and several friends from high school including Beth Moore, Abbey Thomas and Mike Murray. My former coaches Mike Clemente and Walt Ramsey were there, as were some pals from the bar where I occasionally tended, Wendy Rozwadowski, John Garabrant and Jeff Barbilinardo. I do an injustice to all those whose names I cannot list here, but be assured that my heart is with all of you who dedicated your time, effort and funds to that night's success.

Toward the close of the evening, the winner of the 50/50 raffle was read aloud as I was in the midst of a conversation, and it was announced that the woman who had won, Melissa Johnson, chose to donate her winnings back to me. Shortly thereafter, Tom approached the microphone. He thanked the Board of Education, Carmen Amato and Mr. Arnsman, and then asked me to say a few words.

I introduced myself, explained in summary about PSC and its effect on the liver, its degenerative nature, and why I now required a liver transplant. As I spoke, my eyes scanned the room full of faces stopping to make eye contact with as many people I could to relay in the most meaningful way how much this night had meant—that it may have, essentially, saved my life. I pulled a piece of paper from my pocket and unfolded it to reveal a poem I had copied down from a book. I felt under the circumstances that the poem adequately expressed my gratitude better than I could. Just before I looked down, I saw Sue, smiled wide, and then began:

"Success"
To laugh often and much;
To win the respect of intelligent people
And the affection of children;
To earn the appreciation of honest critics,
And endure the betrayal of false friends;
To appreciate beauty;
To find the best in others;
To leave the world a little better;
Whether by a healthy child,
A garden patch;
A redeemed social condition;
To know that even one life has breathed easier
Because you have lived;
This is the meaning of success.[2]

"Because of all of you", I said in closing through my tears, "I have breathed easier. Thank you all from the bottom of my heart". I switched the microphone off and handed it back to Willie, the DJ, then hugged OB, who stood near me during the speech. He and I hadn't embraced since Daddy died.

I took a few cookies from the dessert table and sat down to rest with Mommy and Nana Pawlowski, with whom I hadn't spoken since first arriving. A woman approached me whom I had never before seen and introduced herself, saying that her son wanted to speak to me. As I rose to follow her, my eyes fell on a young boy sitting in a wheelchair

2 Bessie Anderson Stanley, *Success*, 1904. This poem is often credited to Ralph Waldo Emerson with much scrutiny. Arguably, the poem should be credited to Bessie Anderson Stanley, whom I site here.

at a nearby table. Kneeling down I said, "Hey buddy, how you doin?"

"Pretty good," he said, "How about you?"

I said to the boy, not yet knowing his name, "Not too good these days, you know."

"Yeah, I know." he said very simply.

"No doubt you do," I said. "If you don't mind my asking, how do you do it everyday? I have to admit that I sometimes get scared about what might happen to me."

The boy's reply was beautiful in its simplicity, yet perhaps difficult or even poignant for us adults who tend to fret and worry about all the events in our lives. He said, "You can't worry about what might happen or what has happened; just be strong and take each day, one at a time."

I have no idea how old the boy was, or what his ailments were, but it was clear that he practiced this simple belief with each passing day. He had to. He embraced it. He inspired me to embrace it. Our brief exchange did not leave me an emotional mess as I thought perhaps it might, but imbued me with a serene sense of comfort. I knew at that moment that my perspective on illness, and indeed on life, had changed, and I would move into the following day a touch more enlightened than the day before.

After thanking him, and thanking his mother, the evening came to a close. I spent the final twenty minutes saying goodbye to the scores of guests and made my way home with Sue. We were wiped out. Just as we began to settle in, Tom called and asked if we would count the money so he could report it to the Board of Education.

We separated the bills into numeral piles and counted the checks separately. The three of us, my mom, Sue, and me, each took a turn counting and writing down the number to compare with the others. Each time, the total was above $12,000. I called Tom.

"Are you sure??" he said, excitedly.

I replied, "It really is, Tom, and it's all because of you. I can't thank you enough."

I don't recall Tom's response, though I feel certain he downplayed the significance of all he had done for me. That's just the way Tom is, always willing to help and never worrying about what might be in it for him.

Sue and I went to bed after Tom and I spoke. As I lay in the quiet next to her, I began to reflect over the miraculous events of the day. The positive energy was contagious; I knew everyone felt and shared in it. I knew I had come to a turning point, and was ready to take this thing on fully and without fear, taking it one day and one step at a time.

The following morning I received a call from a reporter at the *Ocean County Observer* who had heard about the dinner and wanted to interview me and take photos. Although I didn't care for all the attention I agreed, and later that week someone was sent to the house.

Since I spent most of my time at the computer trying to locate health insurance or researching PSC and liver transplants, the photographer felt it would be appropriate to photograph me sitting at the desk doing research. Chris Lundy, the reporter, called later that afternoon. He asked a myriad of questions about me, the PSC, health insurance, and the spaghetti dinner. He was a great guy, very easy to open up to, fluid in his questions and interactive. I felt as though I were chatting with a friend whom I hadn't seen in a while. The process was not stuffy or formal and was nothing like how I had imagined an interview might be.

The story was printed the next day, on the front page of *The Ocean County Observer*. It was difficult to see a photo of myself, with sunken eyes and terribly jaundice skin. The title read, "Community Rallies Behind Man in Need of Transplant." The story spoke of how the community had pulled together in support of me and described how ill I was. It discussed the rising medical bills and how thankful I was for all the support offered to me through the dinner. It was well-written, descriptive and compassionate. That photo, however, seemed to loom over the article, lending to the tone an air of gloom. Though the previous night's events had filled me with hope, it was interesting to read my story through the perspective of another, however cautiously optimistic that perspective might be. As I gazed over it, I thought, "Wow, I hope I can pull this off."

Chapter 19:
Listed for Life

IT WAS OUR FIRST Christmas without Daddy, and no one was in the spirit to celebrate. Few gifts sat beneath the tree that holiday as the season came and passed nearly without notice.

A few weeks after the spaghetti dinner, I wanted Kelsey to feel rewarded for her act of such tremendous giving, and contacted Santa Claus accordingly. "Santa" then wrote Kelsey a letter, placing inside a crisp, $5.00 bill and praising her for her spirit of good will. Still to this day I smile and am touched by the seamless and unscripted events of that evening. I saw in the eyes of each guest that night the very best of humanity.

Shortly thereafter I received in the mail a letter of approval from Oxford, the health insurance carrier through the State of New Jersey. It stipulated a 30-day limit on the number of days lapsed between insurance carriers. I was charged with the responsibility of proving whether or not this was the case, and dialed the number for the healthcare provider I had while at Fidelity with heavy hands. The woman who received my call was very kind; I was certain, however, that I had far extended past the 30-day mark as I left before Thanksgiving. I felt the weight of my body sink down into my shoes as my heart grew heavy with concern.

What I was about to hear would make or break me. I gave the kind-sounding woman a bit of background information about my health, then said, "I'm trying to determine my last day of health coverage in order to obtain continuing coverage through another carrier." The woman placed me on hold. As the elevator music hummed its tinny-sounding tune through the handset I envisioned her computer and what my personnel files might read. The music ceased suddenly, and she returned to the line.

"Mr. Bonner, I see that you were covered until December 19th."

"Are you sure?" I said, barely able to speak. "My last day with the firm was November 24th," wanting to be nothing but honest.

"Yes, I'm sure. It says so here in your file."

I fell to my knees on my mother's kitchen floor…the same floor upon which my father had fallen as his life slipped away, was the floor upon which I now sat knowing that I had a renewed chance to live. In that instant, with the woman still on the line, I thanked God and also my Dad, whom I'm sure had something to do with it.

"Thank you so much," I said, "You just saved my life."

"No problem, Mr. Bonner. Have a nice day." That news made it an amazing day.

Did the agent change the data in her system? I don't know. Perhaps. She faxed the materials to the state and I quickly called telling them to expect all the relevant information. "That's great," said the representative from Oxford. "There should be no reason why all of your pre-existing conditions would not be covered. I'll approve your application and send your cards out as quickly as I can."

Finally, I could call the HUP financial office and tell them I had coverage sufficient to buffer the costs of transplant, hospitalization and extensive medication. The agent said in response that he would "look into" the details of the plan and return my call when he had finished. It was another instance of feeling that monetary worth outweighed a human life. I had thoroughly researched this particular plan and was certain it fully covered all my costs. Thanks to Tom and the spaghetti dinner, I now also had the money to pay for the high monthly premiums and out-of-pocket expenses.

The phone rang. It was the HUP financial representative. As I listened, my mind began to find his speech unintelligible as he spoke words that I was completely unprepared to hear. "Listen, Dan, I checked out the health insurance plan and I'm not sure that it provides adequate coverage for the transplant. You may need to find a better plan." I was quiet, at first, then it happened: the meltdown. The f-bombs fell like rain and the agent sat quietly on the line without interrupting:

Are you fucking kidding me? I have been busting my fucking ass to find the best fucking insurance so I can get transplanted and you're going to sit there and tell me this plan isn't good enough! Bull-shit! All this fucking time I have been running around trying to squeeze my way into some bullshit plan based on the shit recommendations from the hospital with no fucking luck whatsoever. Then I go and find a good health insurance plan on my own and you're going to sit there and tell me it's not fucking good enough. That's fucking bull shit!

After several moments of extremely awkward silence, he very calmly said, "I know you're frustrated, Mr. Bonner, and I know you are doing your best to find a good plan. Give me some time to research the plan further and I'll let you know." I kept to myself the fact that I now had access to over $12,000 dollars to pay for the out-of-pocket expenses and instead said to him, "Even if you are out of network, the plan covers 80% which leaves me to cover 20% and an out-of-pocket maximum of $10,000. So what's the fucking problem?" I have no idea what color combination arises out of red and yellow; I would think somewhere around orange, but whatever the color result of rage and jaundice, my face was that color.

By this point, his level of calm had risen to an irritated calm as he said, "I'll be able to give you more information once I have the full details of the plan. It sounds all right based on what you are telling me; however, I don't want to mislead you."

It was fruitless to continue yelling at him, and I was filled with regret for verbally assaulting him as ruthlessly as I did. I took a deep breath, ran my hands through my thinning hair and said, "Look, I apologize for what I said. I am just trying to do what I can to get listed and it hasn't been easy. You are a professional. I would like to consider myself a professional and, therefore, I should treat you with the respect you deserve. I sincerely apologize." The conversation concluded shortly after, as I hung up the phone with a heavy hand. I truly felt the plan I had chosen was the best under the circumstances, regardless of what HUP might say concerning its adequacy.

Mommy and Nana Bonner's respective employers both held bake sales in my name the following week, while donations continued to pour in from the spaghetti dinner from those individuals who had either read the news article or could not attend. By the close of both events, there was a staggering $4,000 in additional funding. I was truly humbled by the outpour of good will and in return could only phone the principal of each school to thank them, asking in return if they would thank all who contributed on my behalf.

Several days later, the various pieces of my life's current circumstances fused together cohesively as though by an act of divinity. Seemingly at once I received a confirmation from the insurance company stating that my pre-existing conditions were indeed all covered by the plan, and was then informed by HUP financing that the plan was adequate to cover transplantation. Immediately I scheduled a CAT scan, my last remaining test prior to being placed on the active transplant list. I was fortunate to have the opportunity to schedule it at Community Memorial Hospital, which was located close to my parents' house.

After undressing into one of my favorite frocks, an open-backed hospital gown, the technician framed her introduction to the procedure with, "Are you claustrophobic at all?" I paused. "I am a bit but I think I'll be all right," I said. My will to be placed on the active transplant list temporarily overpowered the fact that I was scared stiff to be rolled into an all-encompassing cold metal tube. "It's pretty tight in there." she said. I wanted to thank her for belaboring that fact but was instead asked to lie down on the tray that would shunt me into the machine. My heart raced and my breathing became shallow—I began to panic and asked to be rolled out so I could have a moment to compose myself. On the second try, I felt assured that I could deal with a few short, albeit uncomfortable, moments in the tube, and once again was proven wrong as I asked to be removed. I sat up on the tray and said, "I apologize for this. I thought I would be able to go through with it that time. There must be some trick to making it more comfortable." The technician responded, "Usually a towel over the eyes seems to work for most people. When they can't see the tube it lessens the anxiety." "Sounds good to me," I said, "Let's do it." With that, she placed a towel over my face and slid me back into the tube. It worked. I thanked her and was on my way, feeling rather triumphant at both the fact that I had conquered a bout of claustrophobia and knew it was now only a matter of time before I would be listed.

I breathed a sigh of relief following the CAT scan and the finale of my precursory testing. So much of my energy up to that point had been drained from me and poured into the battles of the everyday. It was hard to believe that the most difficult test was yet to come—how I would tolerate the transplant, and the long process of healing afterward.

Shortly after my 32nd birthday, I received a call from HUP informing me that I had been officially listed for transplant. I was given instructions to keep my cell phone powered on at all times, that my cell phone should be in my possession at all times, and that I should never travel further than three hours away from the hospital.

One might think that I would have felt tremendously relieved at finally being listed, with my preliminary struggles overcome such as health insurance. The truth of the matter is that after having invested so much in trying to become listed, I put very little mental energy into envisioning what being listed might be like in the context of daily life. Waiting for a phone call on a 24/7 basis was a source of anxiety—I had pressing fears that I receive the call in the middle of the night and fail to hear the ringing—or that I would receive the call, but be stuck in traffic driving and not make it to the hospital. Yet a third scenario was the fear that I would not live long enough to receive a transplant at all.

I began to experience a strange and rather unexpected sense of separation anxiety to my liver. I suddenly felt adamantly attached to it, not wanting to lose it. Though it was obvious that keeping it would kill me, there were periods when I felt that perhaps the most natural way for me to leave this plane of existence was in one piece, the way in which I had arrived. My rational mind told me such thoughts were ridiculous; still, those thoughts persisted for a considerable period of time.

On January 28, 2005, I had an appointment with Dr. Burke. I informed her that I was still able to run just over a mile and was making every attempt to stay active; it was the incessant itching, however, that had begun to take a serious toll on not only my physical body, but my psyche. It had finally reached the point where I felt like it was no longer manageable and I asked for some type of relief. The increase in bilirubin backing up in my system due to the deterioration of my liver was the culprit of the itching. As the liver continued to shut down, there would be a parallel increase in the itching and discomfort. She prescribed Chlorestrymine, a powder to be mixed with a fluid and drank twice daily. After having the pleasure of drinking magnesium citrate on a regular basis for colonoscopies, I was fully expecting the Chlorestrymine to taste deplorable, but it wasn't too bad. Other than a slightly grainy texture, I was able to drink it down with no problem.

The hospital had drawn blood earlier in order to calculate a MELD score for me, which would determine how urgently I needed to be transplanted. Several months ago there was discussion of my receiving a MELD score, but at the time it was not deemed necessary when it was speculated that I may not require transplant for a number of years. My results would not be available during my visit with Dr. Burke, but nevertheless she took the time to give me a more thorough explanation of what the score's impact could be on my transplantation time frame.

She explained that once a person is listed for transplant, several factors would determine where that person fell on the list. For liver transplant patients, each patient's MELD score was the key metric used to determine how critical the need was. While I understood that the scores range from 6 to 40, with 40 being the most critical, what I had not previously realized was that the scores were based within a timeline of three months. There was also a "Status 1" category applied to patients whose life expectancy would be seven days or less if he or she did not receive a transplant. I was *not* a Status 1.

UNOS (the United Network for Organ Sharing) oversees all organ donation activities in the United States. In order to allocate organs efficiently, the U.S. is portioned into regions with each region having its own UNOS center, also known as an organ procurement agency, or OPO (in Philadelphia, where I was listed, the OPO was called "Gift of Life"). All potential transplant recipients are listed within their respective regions. Depending on the organ needed, blood type of the potential recipient, and MELD score (or other metric used for other types of organs), the individual would be listed in order of criticality.

According to a pamphlet published by UNOS entitled, "Questions and Answers for Patients and Families About MELD and PELD" (PELD stands for Pediatric End-state Liver Disease), the MELD score is calculated as follows:

- Bilirubin, which measures how effectively the liver excretes bile;

Gifted

- INR (prothrombin time) which measures the liver's ability to make blood clotting factors; and

- Creatinine, which measures kidney function (Impaired kidney function is often associated with severe liver disease)

The conversation that day with Dr. Burke clarified the entire process and gave me a solid understanding of my status as a transplant patient. She asked if I had any further questions, and normally I would have had many, but on this day I had only one. "Without knowing my MELD score, is there any way to speculate when a liver might arrive?" Dr. Burke then made an announcement for which I was not at all prepared: it was the general consensus among members of the pre-transplant team, without even knowing the MELD score, that I would be transplanted within five-to-seven days based on the severity of my existing symptoms. Excuse me? FIVE TO SEVEN DAYS?

To say that I was confused would be an understatement. I had heard stories of individuals who spent years on the waiting lists and even died because a liver never became available. How was it even conceivable that I could receive a liver in one week?

Dr. Burke explained that my MELD score would likely be greater than 20 and perhaps as high as 25. However, another rather surprising contributing factor was my relatively uncommon blood type. Because livers must be matched to the blood type, having a less frequently occurring type made it easier to receive an organ quickly. Though it sounded counterintuitive to me, it was true.

Lastly, I could be transplanted more quickly due to the number of organs that were available within the region. There would likely be no issue receiving a graft from a deceased individual, making a living donor relatively unnecessary at this point, for which I was extremely grateful. There wasn't a lot left to say at that point. Dr. Burke did her best to assure me that I was in good hands and to be prepared to get that phone call at any time.

Was there a particular time, day or night, that I would be most likely to receive a call? I asked, and Dr. Burke responded that many organs do become available at night, since many donors are victims of car accidents. Hearing that someone had to die in order for me to have a new liver sent chills down my spine. The thought painfully persisted that some poor individual would go about his or her day with absolutely no awareness of the fact that in the next several hours, I would have their liver. It felt wrong.

As difficult as it was to accept, I was forced to finally reconcile within myself that people die every day, regardless of whether or not I was given a second chance at life because of another's death. It was unavoidable. The more I sought out the magic bullet that would save both my donor and myself, the more I realized that even if I were to declare to the hospital, "I've decided I no longer want a liver transplant" it would not prevent that death, or prevent the organs from being implanted into another failing individual who desperately needed them. I had great difficulty accepting this, and to this day it represents for me a sensitive and pensive, complicated dynamic.

I left Dr. Burke's office that afternoon for the long drive home. As I stared at the expanse of highway before me, I tried to envision my future donor, smiling—a fulfilled and joyful person. This thought dominated my mental wandering for the duration of the drive as I prayed for my future donor and the donor's family.

The following day brought the results of my blood work. The pre-transplant coordinator read the results and reiterated to me that based on the data and other symptomatic factors, I should expect to be transplanted within five-to-seven days, just as Dr. Burke had explained. Here are those results:

Liver Enzyme	Normal Range	06/24 2004	08/05 2004	08/07 2004	01/28 2005
Total Bili	0.0 – 1.2	3.5	9.3	8.4	9.8
Alk Phos	35 – 125	712	938	821	1058
AST	17 – 59	129	203	133	189
ALT	21 – 72	181	173	151	179

Chapter 20:
The Wait

SUE AND I FOUND an apartment on the Upper East Side of New York City beginning on February 1, 2005. Now that I was listed, I took all precautions to ensure that my cell phone was with me everywhere I went and set to the highest ring setting. When home, it was constantly connected to the charger. Anxiety began to take its toll on me with each day as I rose with an instantaneous stream of thoughts: Is today the day? What will I be doing when I get the call? Who will call me? What will he or she say? How should I respond? How do I give the word to my family without causing chaos? The best way to alleviate this, I thought, was to have a tightly regimented strategy.

I created a PowerPoint presentation that included the names and telephone numbers (both home and cell phones) for anyone deemed critical, directions to the hospital and the names and locations of several hotels and restaurants in the area. I even listed Nana Bonner and her dirty water dogs as an eating option. Once complete, I distributed it to my family and friends and waited for the elusive but life-saving phone call.

The first weekend after meeting with Dr. Burke, I felt paralyzed. I was afraid to go anywhere or do anything away from home. Hearing, or possibly not hearing the phone ring weighed constantly on my mind to the point of being hyper-vigilant; I trained myself to hear any phone ring even in crowded rooms with tremendous background noise. There was no phone call that weekend.

On Monday, I received a call at 4:30 p.m. Not having had any calls through the day, my heart began to race wildly until I looked and saw it was Uncle Mike. He called simply to check in and see if I needed anything—how I was feeling, what I was doing to keep busy. I truly appreciated his call for many reasons, though especially because it broke the monotony of the long afternoons without Sue while she was away at work. When I wasn't asleep during the day, anxiety wreaked havoc on me mentally and emotionally. Calls from Uncle Mike were most welcome and created a much needed diversion. He must have intuitively sensed this, for he began calling each weekday between 4:30 p.m. and 5:00 p.m. during his drive home. Those phone calls helped pull me through some dark, dark times as I could feel death's grip tighten around me with each passing day. Some afternoons, we talked about nothing in particular; other days, I would spill my guts and tell him just how badly I felt. He always listened patiently and offered encouragement. I hope you know, Uncle Mike, just how much our conversations meant to me.

While the new apartment was being prepared, Sue and I had been staying in a hotel. One afternoon I became restless, and wanting some fresh air, decided to venture out to the apartment to do some cleaning. After only an hour of light activity, I was exhausted. I managed to will myself back to the hotel, where I slept for nearly four hours. When Sue arrived she made dinner and eventually woke me to eat. Sue asked after dinner if I felt up to taking a walk to the hotel gym, which we did, though the only exercise I could do was light running. Nine tenths of a mile passed before I became winded and was forced to walk the other tenth. I refused to quit before reaching one mile—it felt like giving up. The sweat streamed from my forehead, soaking my shirt and legs and causing me to itch uncontrollably. I walked to the vending machine and bought a cold drink, hoping it would quell the sweating, which it did not. I felt so often as though the itching were a living entity unto itself, set against me to devour my flesh, consuming me in this itching, scratching hell from which there was no substantial relief. After Sue had finished, I took an icy cold shower and hoped the chlorestrymine would help. Though it would sometimes take the edge off, it just wasn't enough. I would claw at my body for hours until both my arms and legs bled.

Two days later, I took the subway back to the apartment with the goal of organizing the closets and putting dishes away. As I stepped over the threshold, I realized I was already incapacitated with exhaustion. I called Sue at work with tears burning in my eyes, angry that though I so desperately wanted to help, I simply could not. My body was shutting down more quickly now and there was nothing I could do to stop it. Even though there was no furniture, I piled clothes on the hardwood floor and slept for over two hours before I rose and returned to the hotel, without having unpacked a thing. It was days like that when I felt like a zombie, already dead but still walking.

Seven days had now passed since my being listed, and no call. I wondered if the hospital had already forgotten about me. I prayed they didn't.

That weekend, Sue and I drove together to my mother's house, packed some things I had left behind, and went to bed early Saturday night. Though the temperature in the house was comfortable, I felt my legs and back begin to sweat profusely beneath the covers, as the itching mercilessly ate away at my skin. With both hands I reached down and scraped as deeply and as hard as I could, growing more exasperated with each passing moment. Finally I became so angry that I leapt from the bed, cursing, "This is fucking bullshit; I can't take it anymore!" I found a fan in the next room and set it to blow directly on me, then slept on top of the blankets once the itching lessened to a more manageable degree.

Around 2:00 a.m., the cell phone rang. As I jumped out of bed I said to Sue, "Be ready, this could be the call!" I then saw that it was OB. I was furious. "This better be good or I'm gonna kill him," I thought. "What's up??" I said through clenched teeth. It was clear from his tone that OB had been drinking, and he was quite serious. "I just wanted to talk to you," he said. My anger immediately subsided, realizing that OB was having a difficult time rectifying within himself what was happening to me so shortly after Daddy's passing.

He said, seemingly in one breath, "I feel bad for you; you're my brother and I love you; I wish you didn't have to go through this; I don't want to lose you; you're my best friend and I wish there was something I could do." My heart ached for him — it was the first time I had been forced to stop and listen quietly to the feelings of others concerning my situation. I reassured him as best I could that I would be fine. He continued to talk, and at that point I wanted him to let it all out. In an attempt to lighten the moment, I said in closing, "Listen, I appreciate your calling more than you'll ever know, and I love you too. You're my best friend and the best brother I could ever ask for—but if you call me this late again, I'll kill you with my bare hands." I was heartbroken for OB that night. In order to avoid another crash into panic mode at the sound of the ringing cell phone, I programmed the HUP number to play "When the Saints Go Marching In."

The weekend passed with no word from the hospital. It was now ten days past my appointment with Dr. Burke; desperation followed me like my shadow.

My family became increasingly concerned as more X's appeared on the calendar, with no transplant and no word from the hospital. During my afternoon calls with Uncle Mike, he would occasionally say that if I didn't hear something soon, he would send OB down to the hospital to blow it to smithereens. I could hear the rising concern and frustration in the collective voice of my relatives as they urged me to check in with the hospital and see if there were any complications. I wasn't as quick to unleash a royal inquisition.

Sue asked one evening during our last week in the hotel if I wanted to have one last workout. I certainly did not feel up to it, but agreed in the spirit of pressing on. Six-tenths of a mile passed before I had to stop. I knew that night that pushing myself harder would result in either fainting or vomiting, neither of which was a desirable choice. I began to function with the mindset that my body was losing the fight; my mind was filled with terrifying images of people lying on their death beds, barely conscious. "That could very easily be me," I thought, "if I don't get this transplant soon."

That night I dreamt that I was running on the treadmill, struggling and feeling tired, when all of a sudden I saw Daddy:

"Hey, what are you doing here??" I said, excitedly.

"I came to pick you up so you can come with me," said Daddy.

"Can I come back?" I asked.

"No," Daddy said, "but you can stay with me."

My heart was torn as I gazed at Daddy, desperately wanting to be reunited with him, but also wanting a chance at life to fulfill my purpose here, although I was unsure of what it was or what the future had in store for me.

"I think I want to stay for a while."

"Are you sure?" he said, surprised, "I'd really like for you to come with me."

I said, "I'm just not ready yet—there are things I still have to do."

"I understand." said Daddy, as he began to walk

away, hanging his head and looking as though I had greatly disappointed him. I awoke after the dream in the cool, dark room, disoriented and feeling as though I had completely failed Daddy and let him down.

Three weeks had now passed without a word from the hospital.

Shortly thereafter, Aunt Moe and her husband, Andy were set to fly to China; they had adopted a beautiful little girl. Aunt Moe sent a wonderful card in the mail, apologizing that she would not be in the country for the transplant, but assured me that she loved me very much and would visit on her return. Aunt Moe's words were very touching, and I deeply appreciated her sentiment for me, though I felt it was now likely that I would not see her again. I knew my body was losing the battle.

No longer able to run, I took a walk to Central Park one warm afternoon, with the cell phone in tow. I was despondent and hoped that getting out in the fresh air would lift my spirits. After finding a friendly park bench I watched as children laughed and played all around me. I sat, hopelessly exhausted, thinking of the joyous times of my own childhood and how I wished I could return to them and bring Daddy with me.

When I felt I should start heading home, I realized I was too tired to move, let alone walk the half-mile home. Not knowing what to do, I called Sue. She recommended I sit for a while to see if my energy would return, or take a cab back to the apartment. I figured I would sit for a while but bought a hot pretzel and a soda, hoping to boost my energy temporarily to make it home. As I ate, the sun glared in my eyes, forcing me to close them. Never before in my life had I felt so lonely or helpless as I did on that beautiful afternoon.

I opened my eyes and felt that I had to just go or I would truly never make it home. After forty-five minutes of intermittent walking, I made it. I stopped several times along the way to catch my breath and rest. That afternoon marked the last time I would leave the apartment alone. As I lay on the couch waiting for Sue to come home, I closed my eyes and repeated to myself, "Stay strong and take it one day, one step at a time." I then fell asleep, and was relieved and comforted once I awoke to see that Sue had come home. As we talked that evening she urged me to call the hospital, if not to inquire about my transplant status, then to seek direction. I called on Monday and spoke to the pre-transplant coordinator who scheduled a visit with Dr. Burke, "...provided you are not transplanted by then," she said. I had heard that before.

The day before the appointment, I drove to Mommy's house. She hadn't yet moved her furniture to North Carolina, which afforded me the option to sleep there and more evenly space the trip from New York to Philadelphia. I hadn't slept long that night before a tremendous pain in my back awoke me—it felt as though a knife was being pushed from the front through the back of my body. I took some Tylenol, which was useless, then finally called OB around 11:30 p.m., not knowing what else to do.

He and Jennie were house-sitting at her parents' home

in Beachwood, less than six minutes away. OB insisted I come over and had arranged some pillows and a blanket on the couch while I made the short drive. The pain in my liver was excruciating no matter which position I tried to sleep in. I had to position myself in a way that would alleviate any possible pressure on my liver. I realized, as I tossed and was persistently uncomfortable, that I had to be creative. On all fours, I stuffed several pillows and blankets beneath my torso, aligning myself so that my chest bore the weight of my body. Though it certainly looked uncomfortable, that night it did the job and I slept in relative comfort until morning. I woke and made my way to the hospital.

As I sat in the HUP waiting room to see Dr. Burke, the finance agent (upon whom I had launched a barrage of f-bombs six weeks before) explained that the hospital had wanted to see me transplanted by the close of the weekend. I was furious inside as I was tired of hearing people suggest when I might be transplanted, since it had now been over three weeks with no word from the hospital. Not wanting to unleash another barrage of f-bombs on this guy, I shook my head in disgust and kept my mouth shut.

While meeting with Dr. Burke, she asked a series of questions that were of progressive concern to me the further in-depth they became.

"Do you have trouble dressing yourself, taking a shower, or anything of that nature?" she asked.

"Well, no." I said.

"Can you read a newspaper and remember what you

were reading?"

Unsure of where this was heading I said, "I can read the newspaper."

"That's not what I mean." she said plainly. "When you read the newspaper or a book, are you able to recall what you've just read?"

"Yes," I said, "But reading comprehension was never my strong point."

Dr. Burke then asked, "Do you ever have dizzy spells, trouble driving or difficulty concentrating?"

The persistence of her questions and seriousness of her tone made me feel that something was badly amiss. I explained that though I was having "issues," none of them was listed among her previous questions.

Overall, I said, I felt I was still functioning at a decent level. I had lost a dramatic amount of weight, my eyes and skin were increasingly jaundice, my urine continued to be the color of cola and I was exhausted. Always. All that I really wanted to make a note of that day was the severity of the itching. It had begun to spread to my eyelids and the interior of my ears. It was torturous. I could no longer use the body brush for relief as it simply could not provide a deep-enough scratch. My legs looked as though I had wrestled with a bear and lost. My other issue of concern that I raised to Dr. Burke was my inability to sleep at night, but rather almost entirely during the day. This, she said, was normal under the circumstances.

My symptoms were all perfectly in alignment with those of late-stage PSC. She recommended that I increase the dose of chlorestrymine to twice daily and make an attempt to sleep at night, or at the very least, rest during sleeping hours. Staying awake watching TV through the night, she warned, would only perpetuate the problem. Though I agreed and promised I would try, I knew that it was impossible. Most nights I would lie in bed staring at the ceiling or scratching, eventually giving up to lye on the couch so as not to disturb Sue. After five or six hours, occasionally I would fall asleep.

Dr. Burke also raised the possibility of a disorder called ascitites. My limited understanding of this is that it is a pre-cancerous condition that can manifest in those dealing with long-term PSC. The longer I continued to deal with the PSC without transplant, the higher my risk for ascitites, and the higher the risk for a predisposition to liver cancer. In addition to the potential for ascitites, my kidneys and eyes were also at risk, which explained for me her earlier line of questioning concerning my ability to comfortably read.

I felt an uneasiness that afternoon that I had no recollection of experiencing during previous visits with Dr. Burke. As my battle with the existing PSC grew with each passing day, so too did I now need to find a reserve of energy somewhere within myself to fight off cancer, failing eyes and failing kidneys. My awareness of what it was I was fighting for seemed to fade, lost in the midst of my failing body. I struggled against it, against my own body, and felt at times as though I were schizophrenic or on a see-saw—with my consciousness, the "I" that makes me who I am, fighting daily against my physical body, the vehicle I was sent to this earth in for a purpose. I sat quietly during my remaining time with Dr. Burke.

I did ask, just prior to leaving, why she thought it might be that I had not yet been transplanted. She was vague, but said the hospital was holding out for a highly qualified liver—and one simply had not become available. My fear at that moment was that Dr. Burke could see the desperation in my eyes; I felt she sensed I was giving up and part of me was. It seemed dangerous for me to let this secret out; if the hospital knew I was giving up, why should they go to trouble to secure a liver for me?

While walking through the hospital doors to head home, I felt a maelstrom of emotions: confusion, indignation, concession, anger and sadness. What if no good liver ever came in? Should I just go home and wait for my kidneys to crap out, or go blind? I had no idea how to deal with any of what I had heard during the visit, much less how to tell my family.

Joking, albeit wretchedly bad joking, seemed to be the answer. If I could keep it light enough, I thought perhaps I could shield my family from my inner turmoil. Among those horrid jokes was the possibility of me disguising myself as a doctor and loitering in the ER until someone came in with a B+ blood type and a DNR; then there was the one about receiving a pig's liver or growing a liver in the backyard with liver beans. My two favorites were having OB go in for gastric bypass so I could have a piece of his liver, and once being alerted that a liver was available, drinking wildly all the way to the hospital one last time. None of the jokes was funny in the least and my family was wise enough to see through them and ascertain that I was in fact not handling the situation well at all.

At the time, despite the stress of chronic illness and its tolls both physical and emotional, I considered myself a reasonable, rational person, not easily given to hysteria or flights of fancy and equipped with the limited wisdom of worldly experience…until the night I decided to set my legs on fire. It was the middle of the night when I awoke, drowsy but irritated, looking around the room and wondering what I might do to stop the relentless itching. It was then that I saw the towels. Yes, I thought, if I execute this plan properly, I will successfully scorch away the top layer of skin without damaging the deeper layers of flesh, and the itching will stop. I rose from the bed and began counting all the towels, in order to deduce the number I would need to properly conduct my burning experiment. The goal was to soak the bottom towel layers while leaving the top dry. I would set the top layer aflame, hopefully generating enough heat to scorch, but not melt the skin, then wrap my legs in the wet layer to snuff out any smoking or smell that might wake Sue. I didn't do it—though I very seriously contemplated it. The passing of years and the great human coping mechanism of humor have led me to look back with a light laugh at that moment, though it was an indicator of just how desperate I and my situation had become.

Four weeks had now passed since my initial appointment with Dr. Burke with no word from the hospital. It occurred to me that it may be time to set my affairs in order and begin to transition into a period of focus on family and friends as I prepared to say goodbye. Perhaps this was the way, the only way, to save the life of my donor. If I voluntarily give my life, then perhaps God would consider it an equal trade and let him or her continue living. I had convinced myself that this was the case, and as I prayed, I asked that it would be so.

Aunt Moe and Andy were due home from China that weekend with their daughter, Kimberly, so we planned to meet there to celebrate. It was Saturday, February 26, 2005. I felt quite peaceful, and wanted nothing more than to spend time with Sue and the family. Everyone was there including Nana Bonner, Aunt Marg, Uncle Mike, Aunt Regina, Uncle Tom, Aunt Mary and all my cousins and siblings. Though Aunt Moe and Andy were most likely exhausted from their transcontinental flight, Kim was wide awake and wanted to play. She also wanted to eat and would gladly take a little piece of each treat that was offered to her. She had no fear of being passed around and we each were given an opportunity to make her smile. Uncle Tom, it seemed, was her favorite that day, though she also managed a few smiles for me.

Nana took my hand as we were preparing to leave for the evening and said, "You know, Danny, I pray for you everyday, and hope that you will get a liver soon." As we all did with Nana Bonner, I joked, and said, "I don't think you're doing such a good job, Nana. You'd better pray harder. Maybe you should try actually getting down on your knees." She laughed loudly and said, "Yeah. Right." Nana had severe arthritis and difficulty walking—kneeling was an impossibility. I bent down to kiss her as she said, "I pray hard for you honey bunch, and I love you very much." I said in a quiet and serious tone with my arms around her, "I know you do and I appreciate it. Every prayer helps. I love you, too." Sue and I then gathered our things and left.

It had been the kind of day I was hoping for, one where we all had a great time like a close family should. I was reminded of Daddy's last Christmas and my trip home to spend time with him shortly before he died. I was overcome with a saturating sense of peace and comfort that had been missing in my life for some time.

Later that night I spoke to Uncle Mike, who asked if I had noticed anything unusual about Nana. He told me that after Sue and I first arrived, she broke down, and was taken to another room so I would not see her crying. I knew I didn't exactly look great, but I didn't think I looked so bad as to make Nana upset. According to Uncle Mike, she was afraid I would drop dead any second.

Uncle Tom also called that night, to tell me that he had emailed photos from Aunt Moe's. He warned me that I didn't look well and wanted to be sure I was prepared to see them. I appreciated his concern, I said, but I was fine. As they loaded onto the screen, I was taken aback by the darkened yellow tone of my skin, my sunken eyes, cracked, irritated lips, and emaciated frame. I was unrecognizable, even to myself.

Over the next few days, I spent the hours away from Sue in the solitude of our apartment. I felt a strange stillness as I contemplated what appeared to be the closing period of my life. How should I be feeling? What should I think? Should I be spending more time with family? Should I continue this fight until the last possible moment, or let life take its course and go quietly—or as Dylan Thomas said, "...go gentle into that good night." I had lived a fortunate life with a family who had always supported me in all my endeavors and who made it known at each turn of life that I was loved. Eventually, as I progressed into an increasingly more peaceful state of being, I found myself no longer stressed at the ringing of the phone and never gave thought to when the call might come.

Even at the height of my resignation to what I was fairly sure was the inevitability of my death, a small voice continued to call from the depths of my heart urging me to keep up the fight. I wanted to marry Sue and have children together, watch our kids grow and spend time with family and friends. I missed Daddy—so often in my waking dreams during the long naps that passed the silent afternoons while Sue was away, I felt Daddy was so close; I thought how wonderful it would be to catch up with him and reclaim the year he had missed. We could even, as spirits, sit in the Yankees dugout on opening day and have the best seats in the house. I doubt anyone would mind.

As the one-year anniversary of Daddy's death approached, I felt very strongly that he would not allow me to die at that time. If anything, he would have preferred something extraordinary to happen so that we wouldn't be saddened on the anniversary of his passing. Knowing I couldn't fight anymore, I felt as if Daddy had taken up the fight for me as he wanted me to live. During a regular afternoon conversation with Uncle Mike, I could hear that the concern in his voice had increased after seeing me in person a few weeks prior at Aunt Moe's. He asked as gently as possible when I thought I might be transplanted since it had now been so long. "You know, Uncle Mike," I said, "I don't think anything is going to happen until the weekend of Daddy's anniversary; I wouldn't worry about it."

Though my thinking was certainly unorthodox, Uncle Mike was a master of fireside chats. He had an uncanny ability to listen closely and with tremendous intuition to my words. He responded by saying, "Wow! Wouldn't that be something."

A week prior to the anniversary there was discussion among the family as to what should be done in remembrance of Daddy. There was the possibility of having a mass said in his name, a home gathering, or a small gathering at the gravesite. Given the size of my family, and the complexity of getting everyone in the same place at the same time, it was eventually decided that each should remember Daddy in his own way. Sue and I planned to visit Daddy's burial place and perhaps meet OB and Jennie there at some point during the weekend.

On the Thursday prior to Daddy's anniversary, Sue and I held a special date and called it "Crazy Thursday"...

Chapter 21:
From Ordinary to Extraordinary

I SAW DR. MARKMANN'S lips move silently, as though I were deaf. People flowed in and out of the room doing an EKG and a chest x-ray. The only event I clearly remember is asking Dr. Markmann if I could make a phone call. "Make it quick." he said authoritatively.

I called Sue over at the convent where she had been staying with Aunt Marg. A sister answered the phone and I asked immediately for Aunt Marg, who then put Sue on the phone. A liver had become available, I said, and I had no time to talk for they were rushing me into surgery. There wasn't much to say at that point—Sue said in summary, "I love you! Good luck and I'll see you later."

After talking with Sue, I dialed OB, who had been designated as the messenger to the family in the event that I should receive a liver. He was clearly more than half-asleep as I rattled off in two breaths, "Hey it's me. I'm calling because a liver became available and I'm going for surgery right now. Be sure you tell the family." "Ok." said OB, and hung up the phone.

Within ten seconds, the phone rang. It was OB asking frantically, "Hey! What's going on??" I yelled back, "What do you mean what's going on! I'm going into surgery—they found a liver!" Just then, Dr. Markmann barked behind me, "Get off the phone!"

A resident physician, Dr. Deb (the shortened version of a very long last name) came to my room and began wheeling me to the operating room. As he crossed the nurse's desk, she said in an authoritative tone, "He's not going anywhere since I have no instructions to move him."

Dr. Deb, who until this moment seemed very mild-mannered, raised his voice to a startling tone and said, "He's leaving here right now for a liver transplant, whether you like it or not!" "Damn," I thought, "This guy's got skills." and off we went.

Lying flat on my back with only the minimal amount of pillow for padding behind my head, I watched overhead as we passed swiftly beneath one light then another and another until I saw between my feet the heavy, swinging door to the operating room. The hall was well-lit and warm.

Dr. Deb parked my gurney outside the room and just as quickly was gone. Two women who did not identify themselves came to chat with me, who looked as though they were going to scrub in to the surgery. One asked if I had family at the hospital who might come down to wish me luck before the procedure. I did not, since Sue had stayed with Aunt Marg. It made no difference, really. From my perspective, Sue was with me wherever I went regardless of physical proximity.

Looking under my blanket, the woman asked, surprised, "Where is your hospital gown??" Seeing instead of a gown a grey NYPD t-shirt and a pair of navy blue mesh shorts, she took off running down the hall. After returning, she handed it to me and directed me to the surgeon's bathroom. "After you're finished," she said, "go straight back to the operating room." On the brief walk back to the OR, the drop in temperature was bracing as someone said casually, "Ok, jump up on the table!" I lay down as gracefully as I could with a sore abdomen not knowing what to expect next. It became all too clear to me that I was beginning to unravel as I gazed around the room, knowing that my biggest fear yet would soon come to fruition: catheterization. "Please," I said to Dr. Burke, "tell me it will be done when I'm out." She said that yes, most likely I would be under the effects of general anesthesia. That's good, I affirmed to myself, knowing that it just wasn't going to happen unless I was unconscious. I had to draw the line somewhere, after all. Rectal finger exams, even the ones with a fancy swoop? No problem— well, almost. Fully conscious male catheterization? No fucking way.

A nurse placed a sheet over me. I looked around the room for anything remarkable or worth noting, of which there wasn't much. My classic perception of the OR had been trays of metal tools, a blinding light shining above me and beeps and blips emitting from all corners of the room. There was none of that, but only the simple table upon which I lay, and a few quiet beeps.

I'm in excellent hands, I said to myself. Calm down. As I took a deep breath I realized that my heart was beginning to race, rather than relax. Thoughts about Sue, Daddy, the family and my donor flashed through my mind as my eyes darted around the room in an attempt to find a steady focal point. Two anesthesiologists introduced themselves and told me we would be getting started soon. The "Our Father" came to mind and I sped through it, losing my place and starting over. I followed it with the "Hail Mary" and as I finished, heard the last line resound as though in an echo: "Holy Mary, mother of God, pray for us sinners now and at the hour of our death." My donor is dead, I said to myself repeatedly. That's the only reason this liver is here—so you can live, hopefully. It was as if I had rammed into a brick wall. My heart was pounding so loudly that I looked around the room in disbelief that no one else could hear it.

I heard my vitals announced from off in the distance and knew it wouldn't be long. A nurse loosened the ties on my gown and as the cold air rushed beneath the thin cotton fabric I shivered. "Would you like a blanket?" she asked. I managed to utter the words "No thanks" not realizing until I had to speak how dry my mouth had become. In these final few moments of awareness, all I wanted was to talk to Daddy. "Dad, if you're listening, I need you now more than ever. If you can hear me at all, please look out for me."

With that, an anesthesiologist appeared above me with only his eyes peeking out from beneath his surgical mask. "Ready to get started?" he asked with a chipper tone. With no time to debate the matter, I said I was, but was concerned about receiving gas. It had always made me cough. He agreed to remove it if I began coughing and said, "Ok, here we go." Immediately upon drawing a breath I began to gasp for air and violently cough. True to his word, the anesthesiologist pulled the mask away and waited for the fit to subside.

He asked to try again, and upon my nod placed the mask over my mouth and nose. I remember nothing after that second breath.

My surgery lasted the minimum six hours. Mommy was already in town from North Carolina to finish some final work on her house, with Megan and her kids following behind. Bridget, Jarlath and Ryan flew in from Florida; Uncle Mike, Aunt Regina, Katie, Mike, Jen and John drove from north Jersey; Uncle Tom and Aunt Mary drove from New York and Aunt Jo dropped everything and hopped on the train from Maryland. OB, who was due to work a double shift bartending in Seaside Heights for St. Patrick's Day, left and came to the hospital with Jennie.

After surgery, I would first go to the recovery area and then be placed in the Intensive Care Unit for at least 24 hours. Dr. Shaked informed everyone that they could see me, but to make the visits short. Though I have no recollection of this, I was informed by family that when my surgical gurney was wheeled past the glass windows to the ICU, it was immediately apparent that my skin had returned to its normal tone with no signs of yellowing. After waking when I was told this, I was greatly surprised—since I had been jaundice for so long, I assumed it had stained my flesh and would be days before I returned to my usual pale Irish glow.

I remember slowly gaining back awareness of my surroundings and struggling for a view of the room. My eyes fought me to stay closed. Though I felt no weight, I looked to the foot of my bed and hazily saw a figure sitting there with a hand resting on my leg. My eyes began to focus and it was clear to me that it was Daddy. I felt his eyes on me and felt his presence all throughout the room though my mind had no comprehension of how such a wondrous thing had occurred. My heart beat like a lion. Unable to vocalize my thoughts or move my body, the only demonstration I could give was a few tears trickling down my cheeks as my entire being strained to get up and throw my arms around him. When he saw that I recognized him, he nodded his head and began to be slowly absorbed into the colors of the room. There was no dramatic moment of reaching out to say "Come back!" but a warm and comforting stillness. Daddy was the Constant in life and remained so in death.

Though the room had seemed silent while Daddy was with me those few precious moments, in reality this was not the case. There were at least six people scrambling and preparing various aspects of the room. As I gained full awareness of my body, I felt as though I had been mangled in a train wreck. Despite a long past of chronic illness, I cannot recall an instance of feeling worse than I did at that moment.

"How ya doin, Honey?" a nurse said. I nodded, still unable to speak.

"Ok. Well, I hate to do this to you but I've got to take this tube out." referencing the tube in my nose. She then gave a quick pull and out it came—easily a length that reached down into my stomach. "That feels much better." I said, surprised at how easily I could speak.

"Please don't say that because I have to put it back

in. You don't have a choice." The tube had become coiled in my stomach and required straightening. Although I knew I wouldn't win this battle, I figured it was worth the effort to at least push back a bit. "You know…" I said as sweetly as possible, "I don't even know what that tube is for, so why do I need it?" She then explained that it was in place to prevent anything from passing through my digestive system. She pushed the tube past my teeth and into my throat, at which point I gagged forcefully, feeling sure I would vomit any second. She pulled it out and said, "Ok Hun, try to relax your throat." Despite a concentrated effort, the gagging became more severe, making me feel as though I was losing air and choking on the tube. With tears streaming down my face, the nurse said with irritation in her voice, "I know this is uncomfortable but please try the best you can." I reached up to wipe the tears from across my eyes and said to her, "Can you just hold my hand for a moment? I don't feel well, and I am trying the best I can." Her face softened. She took my hand and said, "Let's try something different this time. I'm not supposed to do this, but I think it will work." It wasn't a sedative, but it did work. She offered me a sip of water and guided the tube down my throat as I swallowed. With that, she laid me down and asked if I felt ready to see visitors. I nodded slowly, not realizing that even had I said no, the door was ready to break free of the hinges from the weight of so many caring family and friends waiting outside. I made it clear that I wanted to see Sue first. As the door opened and she emerged, it was like seeing an angel for the first time.

"How do you feel, Honey?" she said as she kissed me softly on the forehead.

"Not too great." I said, not yet quite in my right mind.

"Why? Are you in pain?"

"Yes, but it's not that. Now that the surgery is over, I have to get a fucking job." Everyone in my family can attest to the fact that I have a terrible habit of swearing profusely after awakening from anesthesia.

Sue laughed. "Oh, Honey, there's no rush for that." She then asked how I was really feeling. I was honest in saying that the pain was above and beyond any stratosphere of pain I had ever felt before in my life. However, there was a pump in my hand that when pushed would release a small dose of pain medicine. The itching had completely disappeared.

Sue was thoughtful of the others who wanted a chance to see me, but before she left I asked her how I looked; I didn't want to further upset anyone as had happened a few weeks ago at the family gathering. To the contrary, Sue said I had regained my color and looked terrific with the exception of some mild yellowing still retained in my eyes. As she pulled the door open, I did my best to emulate Daddy and put on as strong a face as he did following his lung surgery. I worried that I would be unable to hold a comprehensible conversation for long under the lingering effects of the anesthesia.

It seemed as though everyone managed to filter in and out of my room within a span of less than 20 minutes. I remember OB, Bridget and Megan walking in together. OB leaned over and asked how I felt, to which I replied, "I saw Daddy and it was fucking amazing!" They may have believed me, though I have doubts considering that I was still clearly affected by the sedatives and spewing profanity, albeit joyfully. Perhaps they thought it was no more than a drug-induced hallucination.

OB then proceeded to take a photo of my incision with his cell phone. We counted some 67 staple closures (maybe a few less than that) and three tubes protruding from my stomach area. These were in place to drain any fluid away from the wounded area. As I continued to talk with my brother and two sisters I suddenly felt feverish. OB placed a cold cloth on my forehead and stood at my right side. When I turned to look at him and couldn't, I was alarmed, and only later realized that a vein had been re-routed from my leg into my neck to prevent the flow of blood into the new liver.

After OB, Bridget and Megan took their leave to allow the next round of visitors in the room, I remember seeing my cousin Jen and her fiancé John, and later Tooch and Lori. I may have seen many more faces that afternoon, though seeing and remembering as a unified concept was foreign to me as I lay still in a heavily relaxed state. I do recall at one point announcing to the room that I was going to "rest my eyes for a little while," after which I remember nothing but Aunt Mary saying to Uncle Tom, "I just want to sit here with him for a while. I think of him as one of my own." Uncle Tom stood over me and asked if there was anything he could do to make me more comfortable. Though I do not clearly recall asking, I must have asked him for another cool cloth, for once again my forehead was hot to the touch with fever. The last thing I remember is feeling the coolness of the cloth on my forehead and then drifting off for the night.

Six years later, the memories from my life before, leading up to and after the transplant are still so vivid. The sequence of events that eventually led to my transplant are in themselves quite amazing to me, from my lack of health insurance to the spaghetti dinner and exercising my ass off in an attempt to remain strong for the six-hour surgery. Perhaps most miraculous of all is that they culminated on the anniversary of Daddy's passing. This brings me to my final point and that is the often neglected or forgotten power of prayer—for surely it was the prayers of others that sustained me through the most difficult weeks leading up to my surgery.

Sue's parents, Vincent and Claire Donnelly, Mr. and Mrs. D to me, had traveled to a retreat the weekend of my transplant, never suspecting what would happen. When asked if they had any particular requests for others to keep in their devotions, Mrs. D said, "For Danny to get a new liver." Though it was difficult to reach them while out-of-town, someone successfully delivered a message to the priest running the retreat, who announced early that Sunday morning, "We received word last night that Danny did indeed get his liver. He was transplanted yesterday and is doing very well." The congregation went silent for a brief moment as the realization of the news set in and then erupted in thunderous applause.

I was and still am grateful beyond the description of mere words for the support system that sustained me during my long battles with illness. It was never exhausted, for the love of my family and friends that led the charge would not allow it, but rather it always flowed readily, easily and freely. Thus it is that I view the love of others in compassion and prayer to be a reflection of the Divine love within us all.

So, for an ordinary kid born into an ordinary family, I have surely been gifted in an extraordinary way.

Reflections, Acknowledgments and Some Advice

THANK YOU FOR TAKING the time to read my book! From the time I was diagnosed with Ulcerative Colitis to the time I received a life-saving liver transplant encompassed some of the most difficult, painful, gut-wrenching, degrading, physical, mental and emotional challenges I have ever faced. The only experiences more grueling occurred during my time in the hospital after the transplant and the recovery time immediately following surgery. Those experiences and that story are for another time.

I never thought while going through these things that I would one day write a book about it all. After volunteering with organ donor organizations and sharing my story with different audiences, the feedback I consistently received was to write a book about my experience so others could grow from it. I was wary of undertaking such a task, having considered myself to be an ordinary guy who was subjected to unusual and extraordinary circumstances. With enough encouragement from speaking engagements, family, and friends, I decided to give it a try.

This book has been in the making for over four years, three iterations, numerous late nights in front of my laptop, and a thorough final editing. The end result is something I am very proud of. I have joked along the way that it would sell twelve copies with my grandmother buying ten of them. The truth is that if my book sold one copy and it changed that person's life even in some small way, I would consider it a raging success.

This has been a labor of love. It has come together as a direct result of the unyielding love and support from family, friends, medical personnel, and even strangers. I would like to acknowledge some of those people here.

To God, thank you for not giving up on me and for counting me worthy of a second chance at life. Thank you for listening to the prayers of my family and friends, for providing me with strength I did not have, for patience and knowledge when I was confused, and for direction when I was lost. I am now found. I love you.

To my donor, his family, Bill and Cara Haddon and their family, Brian and Judy Warshaw and their family, and all donor families: many times you are nameless, faceless heroes who give people like me a second chance at life. My thanks go well beyond words and extend to the very essence of human nature that we should all be so compassionate and giving toward our fellow man. Your spirits live on inside us and I am most proud to have you as a part of me. I hope we meet someday where I can shake your hand and thank you in person. I love you.

To Dad, I miss you. As time goes on, it seems that the hole left in my heart by your absence gets bigger instead of smaller. There are so many times when I could use your advice, to hear your comforting voice, to feel your arms wrapped around me, or to hear you click your heels and say, "I'm the Constant." My goal in life is to make you proud of me, of the fight that I put up with the same warrior spirit you showed, to show compassion and courage in the face of adversity, and to accept my shortcomings with humility, just as you did. If I can do that, I have succeeded. I am one day closer to seeing you again; until then, goodbye for now. I love you.

To my girl, Susie, I don't know where I'd be without you. There have been more times than I can count where you have been my rock, my friend, my lover, my coach, my motivator, my protector, and my second Constant. You have been my light, my strength, and my resolve. It is because of you that I keep fighting. It is because of you that I can lift myself up when I'm down. It is because of you that I can feel good about myself when I have no reason. Everything I do and everything I live for is because you make me a better person than I ever could be on my own. I am mesmerized by your beauty and find peace in the touch of your hands. There is a special place in my heart for you that no one can occupy nor take away from me. It belongs to you now and forever. You are my guardian angel sent directly from God and I am so thankful to have you in my life. All the love I have goes to you, my girl. I love you.

To Aunt Marg, you have been one of the most amazing people I have ever known. You and I have had some of the greatest conversations I've ever had with anyone. I love the time that we spent together in the hospital as we talked very openly about everything from religion to politics to sports to Napoleon Dynamite. The miracle of you extends deep into your community and the thousands of lives you have touched over the years. You still find more than enough time to share with me and the rest of the family and continue to be a pillar of strength and fortitude for us all. I love you always.

To OB, Jennie, Ownie, and Sophia, thank you for always being there, and I mean always. From late night hospital visits, to my many stays in the hospital, to medical procedures, you guys are wherever I need you to be. OB and I are more alike than we are unalike and with that comes an intense passion for family and friends. You have shown that same passion toward me and I couldn't be more grateful. There is nothing in this world we wouldn't do for each other in a moment's notice or less and I wouldn't have it any other way. You were there for me long before the transplant and I look forward to many more years together. Thank you for your love, care, and support that knows no boundaries. Thank you for the rides in your truck to get ice cream shakes, play cards, watch movies, or play video games. I love you all very much.

To Bridget, Jarlath, Ryan, Liam and Aidan, many thanks for the love and support from a thousand miles away. I can't imagine how hard it must have been for you guys to get information second and third-hand but you never stopped calling, checking in on me, sending me gifts, and making me feel as if you were only next-door. Thank you from the bottom of my heart. I am so proud to be your brother and friend. To the kids, thanks for making me smile over and over and over again. I love you all.

To Megan, Kayleigh, Kieran, and Collin, you never stop and think about yourselves, only about others to make sure they are ok. You and I have teamed up to fight many battles and I'm sure there will be more on the horizon. No matter what, we will always be a team and because of that I can look courageously into the future. Thank you for being my friend, my family, and my strength when I thought I could lose all of those things. To the kids, thanks for making me smile and for pressing my pain killer button when I needed it. I love you guys.

To Nana Pawlowski and Nana Bonner, the two of you do what grandmothers do best – pray. I can't begin to imagine the sheer number of prayers said by you on my behalf and I think God heard every single one of them. Thank you for giving birth to my parents, thank you for being the matriarchs of our families, thank you for the warmth, care, and love that only grandmothers can give. I love you both.

To Uncle Mike, Aunt Regina and family, you guys are always there for me whether it's in Bayonne, Philadelphia, Toms River, Bayville, Penn State, or wherever it is I need a helping hand. I can't thank you enough for all the love and support, the fireside chats, the phone calls at unreasonable hours, checking in on Sue, and helping to keep the family together. I love you.

To Uncle Tom, Aunt Mary, and family, you have redefined "no boundaries" and the miles on your car prove it. You were always willing to take my struggles from me no matter how inconvenient. It was your kids who were in harm's way as the leading candidates for living transplant. I can't express how humbling it is that anyone would go to such great lengths for me. Just know that in the deepest channel of my heart is an ocean of gratitude and love for your family always.

To Aunt Moe, Andy, and Kim, I wasn't sure I'd ever get to meet Kim when you left for China to pick her up. I was so glad that I was around long enough to meet her and play with her that first day in the states. I never knew I would be so fortunate as to have spent so much more time with the family. Thank you for all your love and concern dating back to the time before you gave me the nickname, "Studly." We share a special relationship that extends beyond family. I love you.

To Jo, you have dropped everything on a moment's notice just to be near me. And yet you suffer from your own health problems that no one would ever know about. You are humble and kind and have a bigger heart than anyone I know. Thank you for your love and support and for the conversations we have had that I hold dear. I look forward to more conversations in the future. I love you.

To Mr. and Mrs. D – you have treated me like part of the family from the moment I walked through your door despite the fact that I had flowers for Mrs. D. I thank you for the love, kindness, generosity, warmth, and caring you continue to show me. I am so thankful to have incredible in-laws whom I cherish and admire. I miss you very much, Mrs. D, and I love you both.

To Nancy, Steve, Tara, and Kailey, even though I'm not

even part of the family (wink, smile, Nancy), I feel like one. I appreciate the love, laughter, and good times we share and look forward to when we can get together again. Thank you for all you do for me and for Susie. I love you all and that's what I'm talking about.

To Jan and Bob, "Hey, Man," thank you for being there not just for me but also for Susie when things don't get well for us. I love when we can get together and just be. I hope we all live next-door to one another some day near the beach. That way we wouldn't be so far apart. Thank you for everything now and always. I love you both.

To Kevin, thank you for being real. I thoroughly enjoy talking with you when things seem to be one way, yet you can point me in another. Thank you for the great conversations, book recommendations, stories, laughter, and friendship. I love you.

To the whole Sciarabba Family – who would have thought as neighbors in Toms River that fate had already set us on course to be life-long friends and family. I have asked many doctors what he/she thought the connection could be between John and I and some have responded, "There's got to be something going on there – that can't be just coincidence." Other doctors have said, "It may sound far-fetched but it's probably just a coincidence." Only God knows, but I received a tremendous amount of love and support from all of you, for which I am totally grateful. I love you all very much and know that time and distance cannot break the chains of friendship. For everyone else out there, the next time you have someone move next-door to you, you may want to bake a cake and bring it over to introduce yourself. That family may end up being the best friends you could ever have imagined.

To Dr. Lockchander, Dori, Donna, Arlene and Lindsey, it's hard to believe I've been seeing Dr. Lockchander for over a decade already. In that time you have treated me like family every time I come in for a visit. I appreciate your kindness and sincerity in making sure I was ok. To Dr. Lockchander, they don't make them like you anymore – thanks for staying late for me and for placing calls to your colleagues on my behalf. You all go far beyond the call of duty and I am most thankful.

To the HUP doctors: Dr. Ginsberg, Dr. Kochman, Dr. Makar, Dr. Burke, Dr. Shaked, Dr. Oltoff, Dr. Frank, Dr. Markmann, Dr. Heidi, Dr. Faust, Dr. Reddy, Dr. Axilrod, Dr. Deb, Dr. Dave, and Dr. Taylor; while you may not at all be at HUP anymore, you are some of the most amazing people I have ever met who are beyond smart, beyond skilled, and have saved the lives of countless people. I often find it difficult to express my true gratitude for everything you have done for me but hope that when I shake your hand and say, "Thank you," you know it means so much more. Thank you for saving my life.

To the nurses on the fourth floor of Rhoades: Amy S., Carolyn, Justine, Jessica, Amanda, Dottie, Lauren and Donel. To the very special nurse who took care of me several nights and who brought me McDonald's one night and sugar-free Hershey candy another (I apologize, but I've forgotten your name but certainly not your kindness). To Jim (the nurse manager), and every other nurse at HUP who has looked after me during my many stays at the hospital; you are at times nurses but other times friends, hand-holders, motivators and coaches. I will always be grateful for the tremendous care I get whenever I stop in to have my oil changed and tires rotated.

To Liz Ryan, you are more a friend to me than a nurse. I never thought that our chance meeting in the hospital would turn into such a dear friendship. You are a gift to the nursing profession, providing love and care for those of us who are blessed to have you by our sides. Thank you for all that you have done for me and continue to do. I love you.

To Betsy Knight: Betsy was my first post-transplant nurse whom I met during the morning rounds in the hospital. I can't say anything about Betsy without blurting out, "I love Betsy." She is such an incredible person whose smile and warm heart are absolutely contagious. Betsy gave me huge pick-me-ups with her winks and her smiles during the morning rounds that stayed with me all day. Whenever I know that Betsy is around in the hospital, I have to go and give her a hug. You are an incredible nurse and an even better person.

To Rebecca Farrell: Rebecca was my initial post-transplant coordinator who had to tell me that my numbers in April and May of 2005 didn't look good and that I would need to be admitted. I have kept Rebecca on the phone for hours at times asking questions as reinforced to me that what I was going through was not so unusual. It was unusual to me at the time, and I appreciated her kindness and patience.

I thank you for all the support you give so freely. You are a cherished friend.

To Patti Pfeiffenberger: I met Patti over the phone after she took over for Rebecca, who had gone on maternity leave. I don't think Patti knew the firestorm she was talking to when we first met, but she sure knows now. Whenever we would talk about my liver enzyme numbers, the numbers were usually fine. However, there were times when they were not, and Patti had to talk me off a cliff. Along my journey, Patti has come to know more about my body than any other person on the planet and I apologize to her for that. With that though, it has brought me very close to her. She is a woman I both love and admire. She has garnished the affection of many transplant patients as she now has full-on rock star status during clinic and I have to wait my turn to speak to her. I often call Patti just to say hello and see how she's doing. I'm grateful to have met Patti as she is one of my most favorite people of all time.

To Caroline Pastore, my editor and friend, you are the missing piece to the puzzle of this book that brought it altogether. My book has taken on a new life since you touched it and I couldn't be more thankful and proud of the work you do. You have a gift for words, for telling a story, and for coaching people like me to become a writer when it's probably the last thing on earth I should be doing. Thank you for your friendship, your kindness, and your dedication to my project. I look forward to working with you again. You're the best!

To the Santucci, Steinhauser, Reidy and Greenwood

families, I think it's safe to say that we have moved from friendships to family and I hold each one of you very dear to my heart. Thank you for your love, kindness, and devotion to me and my family through both good and difficult times. You have shown me what true friendship is about, which I am both blessed and honored to share in. My love to you and your families now and always.

Last but not least, to you, Mom: for as long as I can remember, you are the one to whom I went for comfort when I was sick, and that was quite often. You are the one who taught me how to ride a bike and drive a stick-shift; you are the one who took me to the hospital when I broke my finger when I was 12, to have my knee drained when I was in high school and to have the cast taken off my foot when I broke it in college. While my transplant is one of the most difficult things our family has had to endure, we have endured. I am proud to be your son and hope to make you proud of me. I wish you nothing but happiness in life and that I can share in that happiness for many years to come. I love you very much, and not because you gave birth to me but because of who you are and what you mean to me in life. Thanks, Mom.

IF YOU OR SOMEONE YOU know suffers from a chronic illness, I would like to give you some advice that may help you manage your condition from both an emotional and physical perspective:

- Go see a doctor when you think something is wrong. My pride and ego prevented me from taking this critical step sooner, which caused me to suffer pain for a foolishly long amount of time before finally giving in.

- Reduce your learning curve by asking questions— and when you ask questions, keep asking until you are satisfied with the answers. The doctor cannot read your mind, so let him or her know very clearly your concerns. If you would like to further educate yourself about your disease, ask the doctor for some recommended magazine articles, internet websites, or other reference tools. If your physician seems unwilling to do this or to readily answer questions, you may want to consider seeing another doctor.

- Trust your gut instinct. If something doesn't feel right, say something. If you don't agree with how you or your disease is being treated, say something. I have no idea why the first gastroenterologist I consulted was so uncomfortable around me, but it made me uncomfortable. I never said anything to him, but in retrospect I wish I had.

- Find a support group. If you can't find one, ask your doctor for information. If that doesn't work, email me at dbonner73@hotmail.com. I don't care what type of disease you have—I enjoy talking to people about whatever condition they may have, exchanging some hell stories, and offering support in any way I can. I do this because I was fortunate to have an unyielding support system in the form of my dad and later the rest of my family, whereas others may not have such luck.

- Follow the golden rule of being healthy: eat right and exercise. I know, it sounds cliché but your body simply works more efficiently when you treat it well rather than abuse it. I know there will be days when you can't run, lift, or even walk to a degree with which you are satisfied, but don't give up. Do something—anything. Find a partner who will motivate and exercise with you. I personally believe that working in unison with your mind, body and soul can make all the difference in how your disease progresses and how well you will fight, mentally and physically.

Good luck! I'm here if you need me.

About the Author

Dan Bonner currently lives in Bayonne, NJ, with his wife, Sue. They both work in the financial services industry and are active volunteers in their church and within the transplant community. Dan would one day like to travel the country conducting public speaking events as a motivational speaker and advocate for organ, tissue, and blood donation. He would also like to open his own financial consulting business. Sue would one day like to own a small coffee shop that serves breakfast and lunch. They enjoy day trips to the Jersey shore throughout the year.